FAIR SKIES AND TIGHT LINES

MIKE YURK

authorHOUSE®

AuthorHouse™
1663 Liberty Drive
Bloomington, IN 47403
www.authorhouse.com
Phone: 833-262-8899

Published by AuthorHouse 10/31/2024

ISBN: 979-8-8230-3218-6 (sc)
ISBN: 979-8-8230-3217-9 (e)

Mike Yurk
415 Valley View Road
Hudson, WI 54016
bassinmajor@yahoo.com
715-381-6505

Dedicated To My Friends in The Writing Business

Art Dumke

Kate Erbach

Dena Gervasi

Ann Littleson

Paul Smith

April Tesch

With special thanks to

Robert Darragh

For giving me the title for this book

CONTENTS

THE LITTLE HOUSE OUT BACK

It's an outhouse. You do not see as many as you once did. Thanks to modern day technology most cabins, shacks, and hunting and fish camps today have running water, showers, flush toilets and the other luxuries of today's world. But it wasn't long ago when outhouses were the norm rather than the exception; especially it seemed when you went "up north" when I was growing up in the 1950s and 60s.

In those days there were still homes, usually in rural northern areas, where flush toilets had not yet arrived. When I was a kid, I had an aunt and uncle who lived near Amberg in northeastern Wisconsin. My uncle had a small herd of beef cattle and they lived in the woods for the most part. It was always an adventure to visit them. They had a hand pump for well water in their kitchen and although they had electricity, they did not have a flush toilet.

They had an outhouse out back and in the silly way kids are, it seemed "neat" as we said then. It is only as I have gotten into my sixties when I now need to use the bathroom three or four times a night, I realize how unpleasant those nightly trips to the outhouse must have been, especially when winter temperatures got below zero. Both my aunt and uncle have passed away and their little farm was abandoned. A few years ago, I drove past their old farm and their house and the sheds out back were still there and so was the outhouse.

Again, in the days of my youth, I remember stopping at a small store or gas station in the backwoods areas of northern Wisconsin and when asking where the rest room was, I was directed to an outhouse behind the store. That's the way life was then and had been for long time.

Waste disposal has been one of the great problems men has wrestled with from the dawn of time. When people began to live in cities getting rid of waste became critical. Many of the great plagues in the Middle Ages were a direct result of too many people living too close together with no place to get rid of their waste. I once recall seeing a castle in Germany with little outhouse type rooms hanging over the moat. The waste was then deposited in the moat. Can you imagine how that moat must have smelled on a hot summer day?

Throughout history entire military campaigns were lost not because of weapons or tactics or armies or military leaders but by not disposing of waste. During our own Revolutionary War, the Battle for New York failed in a no small part because our soldiers were getting incapacitated from various diseases resulting from indiscriminate waste disposal.

I do not know when the first outhouse was devised but for centuries that is all the world had. Modern sewage systems and septic tanks we know today have been in existence since somewhere toward the end of the nineteenth century.

George Washington's home in Mount Vernon had outhouses. In its day it had all the modern conveniences of its time but they had to use an outhouse. I saw our first president's outhouse when I visited Mount Vernon a few years ago. It had three holes so he could take care of business and conduct business with two of his advisors at the same time if he needed.

Originally all houses in the civilized world had outhouses. Even the White House once had outhouses. When Abraham Lincoln was in the White House there was a row of outhouses on the east side of the building. I wonder if the president had one specially designated for his exclusive personal use or was it first come, first serve for everyone.

All of our large cities such a New York, Chicago and all the others had outhouses out back of residences. Today there are people digging in the locations of those outhouses to find artifacts from those old days to tell us how people lived then. It is amazing to see the things they have pulled out of there. As our country expanded west, outhouses were part a distinct part of that movement. Looking at any of the old photos of the west you can see outhouses throughout the boom towns of those years.

Today, of course, we have all those modern waste disposal systems such as municipal sewage systems for cities and septic tanks for the country folks. They truly are marvelous. In one city of about fifty thousand people sitting on the banks of the Mississippi River the sewage department takes in the waste, separating the sludge from the liquid. The sludge is stored and provided to farmers for fertilizer while the liquid is treated and within less than a half day is deposited in the Mississippi River cleaner then the river water itself.

For people, who like me live in the country, we have septic systems taking my family's waste, again separating the sledge from the liquid and eventually dispersing liquid waste through a drainage field in my backyard without contaminating my water well. This may seem simple but it is not and having a reliable waste disposal system and fresh, clean water at the same time in our country is a luxury many people in the world do not have. I have been to a number of countries where water is contaminated from poor waste disposal and you dare not drink the local water or you could spend a lot more time in the outhouse.

Although we have these modern waste disposal systems in our country, outhouses are still a necessity both in our country as well as around the world.

In northern Minnesota I go to a fish camp for the opening weekend of their fishing season and later in the fall for another weekend of fishing.

Although we may have a television with a dish so we can watch sports (Hey we are guys. What would you expect?) the rest of camp is rustic. We get our water from a hand pump and we have an outhouse. The outhouse had to be rebuilt a few years back and it was a lovely piece of construction.

In the true tradition of outhouses in fish camps all across the Northwoods, it has pin ups on the wall and even a bracket holding a small library of magazines. That was a nice touch. Once a group from the camp discussed adding running water, a shower and a flush toilet until someone pointed out that could possibly encourage women to visit the camp. There was a long moment of silence as everyone pondered that and then someone changed the subject and improving the camp was never brought up again.

There are some outpost cabins on fly-in fishing trips in Canada where we have found showers and even running water with the help of solar powered pumps. Now the water isn't drinkable since it is taken straight from the lake but we can always boil or filter water from the tap. It is nice not to drag buckets of water up from the lake and even to take an occasional shower. However, we still have the outhouse. In one camp there was even two outhouses. That was especially luxurious. The outhouses were loosely constructed allowing air to blow through. This was beneficial to reduce any odors but also permitted the bugs easy access to those sitting in the outhouse. This certainly reduced lengthy stays in the outhouse which did not permit a lot time for reading while in there.

Another camp in northern Minnesota was once a friend's family homestead. When it was originally built in the early 1900s it had an outhouse. During the winter, when temperatures have dipped to twenty below and colder, we don't see anyone having lengthy stays in the little house outback. My friend's family ran a power line to the outhouse to installed a small electric heater but when it is twenty below zero it helps only minimally. Even with that, it doesn't encourage lengthy stays.

When I was in Desert Storm in Saudi Arabia, I stopped at what was called a Convoy Support Center somewhere between Riyadh, the country's capital, and the Iraqi border. It was a sparse grouping of tents consisting of tents for sleeping, a mess tent providing food and beverages twenty-four hours a day, several fuel tanks and a long row of outhouses. They did not dig trenches under the outhouses but instead cut fifty-five gallon barrels in half. Half of the barrels were slid under the outhouse. Once they were full, they were pulled out, gas poured in them and lit on fire to burn off the waste while the other half of the barrels were slid back under the outhouse. It was effective and worked but I imagine there weren't a lot of volunteers for the burning detail.

On several of the lakes, such as Red Lake in northern Minnesota, sleeper ice houses are rented. The idea of having a sleeper ice house is so you can ice fish all day without having to leave the ice. You sleep there and your ice house becomes a little cabin. No one wants to leave the ice to go find a bathroom, especially when the fish are hitting, so outhouses are provided on the ice.

There will be a cluster of sleepers with a single outhouse located close by. They are designed similar to the ones I encountered in the desert.

There is a half barrel inserted under the seat, lined with plastic bags. Every day or so someone comes out to remove the full bag which is eventually disposed later on shore, replacing it with an empty one. When it is below zero the temperatures discourage lengthy stays and no one seems to take a magazine in there with them.

In a lot of places today we have the modern version of the outhouse in portable potties. We find them whenever you have a large group of people at any outdoor activity such as state fairs, ball fields and others. I find them often at boat landings and in parks. The waste is deposited in a holding tank which is periodically pumped out while adding a new supply of toilet paper.

I have one memorable outhouse experience. My company was deployed to a large, barren air strip in Turkey near the town of Corlu on the European side of the country. We were there for an exercise and once it was over everyone else were transported out except my company. We were held there for a couple extra days, waiting for our airplane to take us back to Germany. One morning I was sitting outside our tent when one of my sergeants went over to use the outhouse. The outhouse was a row of individual outhouses nailed together. Contractors came in before the exercise started, dug the trenches for them and placed the outhouses on top as well as setting up the camp with large tents. The contractors were now dismantling the site, dropping and folding tents and getting ready to put everything in storage until the next year for this particular exercise. I forgot about my sergeant until I saw a contractor driving a forklift over to the outhouse, pick it up and drive off. I jumped up and started running after him, yelling at the driver to stop. I finally got his attention and got him to lower the outhouse and back off. The door opened and my sergeant stepped out with a bewildered look on his face. I didn't ask him if he was finished using it.

Even with all the modern improvements in waste disposal, outhouses or their equivalent portable potties are here to stay. There are places where they are just as important as they were hundreds of years ago. Besides it is hard to imagine a hunting or fishing camp without them where the iconic outhouse is part of the adventure.

VINTAGE FISHING

I collect old fishing equipment. I guess it started when my grandmother gave me my grandfather's gear after he died. He left me about half a dozen old rods with metal level wind casting reels, his old tackle box and his deer hunting rifle. This was shortly before I joined the Army and left on what would become a twenty-year career. During those years I moved ten times but through all those moves I kept grandfather's old gear.

Grandfather's rifle is now in my gun safe and his fishing gear sits on the base of the fireplace in my family room with a lot of other gear I have collected since.

After retiring from the Army and settling down in Hudson, Wisconsin, I had room and time to collect more vintage fishing gear. I found old rods and reels in antique stores and junk shops. Some friends, knowing I collect that stuff, gave me more old rods or reels which were sitting in their basement or corner of their garage.

In addition to rods and reels I started picking up old baits. Many of them I remembered from my boyhood in the 1950s and 60s. I recall looking at them in the sport shops and hardware stores. In those days most hardware stores also sold hunting and fishing gear. As I look back it seemed to me many of those sport shops and hardware stores, especially the farther north you went, were dark and dusty. I suppose when you are selling grass seed and fertilizers in the same store with fishing gear it would be a bit dusty. Even the sport shops seemed dark and dusty. I don't think dusting was a priority for owners in those days.

In the stores I looked at all the baits, usually hanging from pegs on peg boards or sometimes swing out boards attached to the wall. I loved to look at the baits and dreamed one day I would own a bunch of them. The dream was hard to realize in those days with my allowance and the occasional grass cutting job, but dream I did.

I remember two sport shops. One was on a back street in Oshkosh and I think I recall the place was call Matt's. The other was a sport shop in Sheboygan. Both stores had large front windows where they laid out a number of plugs (we call them crankbaits today) and other baits. I loved looking in those windows.

Back in the day there seemed to be a lot of different baits but there were relatively few in comparison to what you find in today's bait shops and fishing stores. They were packed in card board boxes with such names as Heddon and Cisco Kid. The one I remember the best was the River Runt. For collectors today, the boxes are worth as much and, in some cases, more than the baits themselves. That seems strange to me. If you can find both the bait and the box together so much the better.

Many of these baits are no longer made. The Cisco Kid is now owned by Suick and they do have a Cisco Kid Topper still in their inventory but the rest of the Cisco Kid baits are gone. The River Runt is also long gone. It was one of the first baits made with plastic. Most baits prior to World War Two were made from wood but plastic became more popular in the late 1950s.

My bass fishing buddy, Scott Clark of Hudson, Wisconsin, and I discussed, over the years, as to whether any of those old baits could still catch fish today. Many fishermen theorize fish eventually become used to certain baits and when they do they catch fewer fish. If that is the case, then many of these older baits have long passed out of the collective memory of today's fish. With that in mind, Scott and I set aside a day every season to fish with vintage gear to test our theory whether these old baits still work today or perhaps in some cases even better than some of our modern baits.

In keeping with the vintage theme, I have a replica of an old wooden tackle box. It is easy to forget, today with the modern plastic tackle boxes and soft sided tackle bags most tackle boxes were first made of wood and later metal. I remember my father having a metal tackle box with the bottom of the trays lined with a thin sheet of cork. I still have my grandfather's metal box and it retains the comfort smell of fish and oil for his reels and outboard motor I remember so well. My wife, Becky gave me a wooden tackle box for Christmas one year and I knew instantly I was going to use it as my vintage tackle box.

The box is filled with baits which are no longer available. I have some River Runts and Cisco Kids as well as several other baits from the 1950s and 60s. As well, I have some newer baits which are no longer made. I also have some baits, although still manufactured, are no longer made in the colors I have. It is something of an eclectic collection. My grandfather's old fishing knife is also in the box. That knife is probably fifty years old.

To add to the ambiance of the day, we fish with old rods and reels. That started a couple years ago when I was in an antique store and found a Ted Williams spinning rod and reel. Although Ted Williams is known for his baseball career with the Boston Red Sox, he was also a big outdoorsman and after retiring from baseball became a promoter for Sears and Roebuck sporting goods. I well remember seeing Ted Williams rods and reels, guns, tents and other items both in their catalog and in their stores when I was a kid. I got that old rod and reel for thirty dollars and it was blast from the past for me when I bought it.

I noticed it still had old yellow monofilament line on it and it got me thinking. Why don't I put new line on it and try fishing with it again. I imagine that old rod has probably not been used in over thirty or forty years. I put new line on it, taking it with me the next time I went bass fishing and used it for about an hour before I switched back to my modern gear. In the hour I fished with it I caught four or five bass and felt a mixture of joy and nostalgia while using it.

Over the years I have been collecting old Mitchell 300 reels. The Mitchell 300 was the first spinning reel I owned as a kid when I finally could afford to purchase one which fostered a soft spot in my heart for them ever since. They were big, heavy reels but rugged. They were indestructible which is why they are still around and work today. I rummaged around my basement and found some old fiberglass rods from back in the 1960s and 70s which I found in junk shops or people gave to me. I matched those rods with the Mitchell 300s. It took me back to early fishing days and they were not only a great memory but fun to use again.

Now when Scott and I go on our vintage fishing day we use old baits on old rods and reels. For the day I also wear a straw hat. When I was a kid, I remembered all the old fishermen seemed to have one. It wasn't just any straw hat but one with the front of the brim cut off, replaced with a green plastic piece like a sun shade. I looked for one for a number of years. Some people told me of a store or two they thought still carried them but when I check they didn't. I thought I might find one in a junk store but I didn't find any there either. One December when I was in Key West, Florida, I found a pile of them in a store. I searched through the pile for one which fit me and bought it. I wore it on the flight home to walk out of the airport in Minneapolis, finding snow on the ground.

The day is warm and sunny. Sunlight dances off the water. It is a great day to go fishing and a great day to use vintage gear. Scott jokes we didn't need to go to a sport shop to go fishing today; instead, we went to the antique store.

We start fishing right from the boat landing. We are fishing over deep water with a thick mass of weeds on the bottom. I start with a Lazy Ike. It is a color Lazy Ike no longer offers. I remember I bought this bait from a hardware store in the Oshkosh in the mid 1970s. The store is long gone now like many of those baits they sold then. The bait is not running right and after several unsuccessful attempts to tune it I finally put it back in the tackle box and switch to a Heddon Sonic.

One of my fishing buddies told me Sonics were one of his father's favorite baits in the 1960s so I found some on eBay and bought them to add to my vintage collection. I try them in a couple of different colors for about twenty minutes and never got a strike. I guess today is not a Sonic day. I will try them some other time and feel reasonably assured they will work another time. I switch to a yellow River Runt. It doesn't run right so I take it and put on another one in the same color which seems to work fine.

Scott catches the first fish. He catches a foot long bass on an orange spoon with black spots. I know spoons are still sold today but Scott's spoon is somewhat unique as it has two small spinners at the bottom of the spoon. I remember them from the 1960s and 70s and I haven't seen them since. He got it from his father's tackle box. It also brings up the question as to why today's bass fishermen do not use spoons more often. With all the other baits out there, spoons may be a much over looked bass bait.

A few minutes later I feel a fish slam my River Runt. It puts up a frenzied fight and a couple moments later I see a thin shadow in the water. It is a northern pike. I switch to a perch-colored River Runt and a few minutes later catch another northern.

I switch to a lure called The Charmer. I found several of them in a junk shop in Oshkosh some thirty years ago. The junk shop is now a sandwich shop. One of the interesting things about buying and using old lures is to research them. The computer and internet help a lot. I did a Google search on The Charmer and found they were made by the Hunt Lure Company and billed itself as "The King of Bass Lures." Dewey Hunt was making and selling these lures out of his gas station in the early 1950s and by 1960 started to make the lures full time. By the late 1960s the company was out of business but in its day, they made two other baits plus The Charmer.

The Charmer does not run right and after trying to tune it I give up and change to a Cisco Kid. As we fish, Scott and I talk about these old lures. It seems at least one out every two we try doesn't seem to run properly.

We recognize many of these lures are forty years old or more. Perhaps they lost their action simply because they were fished a lot and are now too beat up.

But some baits seem to be working just fine and one of them is the Cisco Kid I now am using. It is a plastic bait with a metal lip probably from the 1960s. A slip of paper in the box tells me it is a "Proven Killer For …. BASS, WALLEYE, TROUT, PIKE and many other game fish."

On the box it also claims to be "America's No 1 Fish Getter." On the first cast I see a flash in the water but the fish misses the bait. A couple casts later I feel a solid strike and set the hook. The fiberglass rod I am using is doubled over as the fish races off but I quickly turn the fish and get it coming to the boat. A moment later I pull the fish in the boat. It is another northern pike.

I enjoy fishing with old spinning rods and reels but notice these old rods are much heavier than those we use today and much softer which makes it harder to set the hook. I know we used those rods for a lot of years and marvel at how many fish we caught with them in spite of their drawbacks in relation to the rods we use today. Also, after a day of fishing with the older, heavier rods I can feel it in my shoulders which I never remembered years ago. But then I was a lot younger too.

I stick with my Cisco Kid and see a number of fish chase it. Every now and then one hits it hard enough for me to set the hook. The other thing with the older, softer rods is they bend a lot further when a fish is fighting against it which is exciting.

Scott is switching between his favorite modern baits and the older baits but doesn't seem to do any better with one over the other. Maybe the old baits are just as good as our modern lures.

Finally, I catch a bass. It is a foot long fish and puts up a good fight. The soft rod is bent in half and the rod tip is plunging. I get the fish into the boat and release it.

We fish until late afternoon and by the end of the day we caught fifteen fish; nine bass and six northern pike. By any standards, whether it be today or forty years ago, it is a good day of fishing.

The old stuff still works and a day with an old Mitchell 300 reel or a Ted Williams spinning outfit and River Runts and Cisco Kids brings me back to the days, the memories and dreams. I enjoy the memories and days of fishing from the past and the dreams I once had. My dreams have come true and more, so I have been lucky and fishing vintage gear reminds me of that.

THE SONG OF SEPTEMBER

There is something special about September. It really isn't summer but it isn't fall either. It is a bit of both. This is the Song of September. You hear it in the wind through the trees and across the waters. It is a song of change as one season leaves and another begins.

In September you leave for fishing in mid day and have the air conditioner on in the car, then to return home in the evening with the heater on. You will see the first colors on the trees. The bright red colors of maples and sumac tell of the coming autumn. Everything seems to be changing in September.

When I was growing up in the 1950s and 60s Labor Day seemed pivotal in my young life. Usually, the last grilling out of the summer was during Labor Day weekend. Life seemed much more regimented then. You only grilled out in summer. The grill normally came out on Memorial Day weekend and then got packed away in the garage or basement right after Labor Day. That meant you had all winter long to think about how good a grilled hamburger or bratwurst would be.

Also, the day after Labor Day was always the first day of school and once again, we would be standing outside waiting for the yellow school bus to pick us up. It would be a long nine months before we got off the bus for the last time of the school year for summer vacation. Normally we started out wearing short sleeve shirts but by the end of the month we were in sweaters and jackets.

Despite the unpleasantness of having to return to school I liked the month of September. After the dog days of August, it seemed fishing flourished again. Possibly it was the first cool days and nights of September that turned fish on. In October hunting seasons started and people forgot about fishing then so the unofficial end of the fishing season normally ended with September.

In my youth, September was about trout fishing. It was the last month for trout fishing and my father and I tried to get every opportunity we could to go. Labor Day weekend was our last trek to the far northeastern counties for brook trout. Then we spent the remaining days of the season fishing near Wautoma for brown trout.

There was a lot to like about September trout fishing. There weren't any bugs which is always nice. Temperatures were cooler making it pleasant to be wearing waders after the hot days of August. There were few if any fishermen out on the streams. Father and I wondered why no one else was on the streams in the last month of the season. For my father and me we couldn't get out enough in those last weeks. It was the best fishing of the season after May. And we had it all to ourselves

For sure we always got out on the last Saturday in September which was my last chance at trout fishing. By late September it was cool even during the middle of the day. My father's favorite stream was the Mecan and we parked on the road, rigged our spinning rods and then hiked to different spots on the stream.

It seemed magical to slide off the banks into the water. It rushed around my legs, tugging at me. We fished spinners for trout then and I worked upstream, flipping my spinner into holes, past brush and around logs. Occasionally I was rewarded by having a trout dart out and slam my bait. It was a quick, intense struggle to finally get the fish into the net.

I never broke a sweat for most of the day and felt a sense of satisfaction as I walked along the road back to the car with a creel bulging with trout. In those days the limit for trout was ten fish and you could always expect a good half a dozen trout for the day and some of them would be around a foot in length. When I was in junior high school and then high school my season ended on the last Saturday in September. The next day was Sunday which was reserved for church and then back to school on Monday. The trout season actually ended on the last day of September which was often in the middle of the week. I wasn't able to participate in the actual last day of the season but Father did.

Later when I was in college, I had a bit more freedom in my schedule so I joined Father on the last day of the trout season. We got back to the car usually in the early evening as shadows were getting longer. We dumped our fish in the ice chest and looked at them, knowing we weren't going to get any more trout for the next seven months until the new season started again in May. In the last year or two, before I joined the Army, Father and I would split a small bottle of champagne on the last day. Leaning against the fender of his car we clinked our glasses together in a toast to the end of another great season. As we sipped our champagne, we were reluctant to leave. We didn't want the day to end and we relished listening to the final notes in the Song of September.

That was over forty years ago. I do not trout fish much anymore. Instead, I bass fish and much like the trout fishing I found in my youth, September is a great month for bass fishing too. Bass fishing in September has many of the same qualities I remember from my day's trout fishing; no bugs, cooler weather and fewer people on the water. It just might be the best month of the season for bass and I know I have caught a lot of big fish in September. I still continue to hear the Song of September.

It was mid-September and the first big storm of the season was pounding us. My buddy, Paul Valle of Cumberland, Wisconsin, and I were sitting at a landing looking out across the water at the lake we planned to fish. Bruised, black clouds were piling up on the horizon and the wind whipped the lake into froth covered white caps. Although not a particularly big lake the water looked intimidating and we would be launching the boat right into the wind. We hated the thought of giving up on the day but this lake did not look promising. Finally, I said something about it not being worthwhile to fish this lake today. Paul reluctantly agreed. Then I mentioned just north of us about twenty miles or so was another lake. It was smaller so perhaps the wind wouldn't be so bad there and we would be launching with the wind rather than against it. It had been a couple years since I last fished it but it looked like the best alternative to saving a day of fishing.

As we were launching the boat, we noticed the storm followed us but it wasn't raining yet. I made a comment perhaps the rain would hold off for a few hours while we were fishing. Within the first dozen casts my bait jolted to a halt. I felt a fish pulling back. The fish tore off but I turned it and got it coming towards the boat when it ran off again. Finally, I had it alongside the boat and Paul brought the net up underneath it. It was a fat seventeen-inch largemouth bass.

After releasing the fish, I looked over my shoulder. Dark clouds were rolling in. Paul and I anticipated the worst and were already in our rain gear.

We were hoping it wouldn't rain but were realistic enough to expect it. Suddenly it started to pour. There wasn't any light rain or sprinkles to start and instead it was like someone opened the water faucet. The wind picked up as quickly as the storm blew in. We pulled up hoods, turned our backs to the wind and just continued fishing.

We worked along the shore and steadily caught fish. The fish hit hard and fought with reckless abandon. It was like the storm charged them. Drags on reels gave out line and spinning rods were doubled over with rod tips plunging as fish race off. We felt battered by the rain and wind. Later Paul told me he wished he had taken a photo of me with the water streaming off my hat. I caught a twenty-seven-inch northern pike. It is a nice bonus to the day.

At the end of the afternoon, we were in a marshy corner of the lake just beyond the landing. We agreed we would fish this last spot and then head in. The rain continued without let up and by now had worked its way through the rain gear and was soaking into the clothes nearest our skin. Paul yelled. He had a fish and it felt big. I reeled in my line and grabbed the net. The fish raced off swirling on the top of the rain splattered water. At the boat the fish pulled away several more times before I got the net under it. It was an eighteen-inch bass and the biggest of the day. It seemed like the right moment to quit. Back at the landing as we were strapping down the boat the rain began to subside. Dark clouds still swirled overhead but the rain stopped as suddenly as it had started. We laughed. "It figures," one of us said.

Although it was turbulent and sometimes harsh, the storm seemed to turn on the fish so we didn't complain about the weather and just enjoyed the adventure. Even in the rain we heard the Song of September

A week later I was on the upper St. Croix with another fishing buddy, Scott Clark of Hudson, Wisconsin. The day was cool and overcast. The trees showing color stood out brightly against the other trees still green and the slate gray skies. "We are looking for deeper water with current close to banks," Scott said to me. He pointed to one stretch of shore and I angled the boat toward it.

Scott is fishing a plastic rig and in the first ten minutes he boats three smallmouth bass, each about a foot long. I am using a crankbait and it took a few more minutes before I felt a fish slam my bait. It put up the no holds barred fight typical of smallies. The fight never ends for these fish as they are still fighting as you net them. By the time we finish that stretch of bank I had six smallmouth bass.

We move upriver and let the wind and current drift us along another spot of deep water adjacent to a rocky bank. Scott picks up a northern pike. We try a couple of other areas and I lose what looks to be a thirty-inch northern pike.

Scott picks up a walleye. It is the only one we caught that day. It begins to rain and we put on rain gear but it is a light rain and does little more than irritate us.

We move back to the first stretch of water we fished and as we are drifting along, I see Scott pull up on his spinning rod. His rod is bent in half and I can hear the drag on his spinning reel whine as it haltingly gives out line. It looks and sounds like a big fish so I get the net. I am waiting as Scott continues his tug of war with the fish and then I see it in the stained river water. It is a big smallmouth. Now we both are getting excited. The fish sprints away and again Scott gets the fish coming back to the boat. I get the net out but the fish darts off again and again and again but eventually Scott pulls it close enough to lead it into the net. As the net clears the water the fish is still thrashing in the mesh. The fish is a fat nineteen inches.

We hit a couple more points and pick up two more fish by the time we quit. Our total fish count with the northern and walleye is twenty. It is later in the month and we can feel the edge of fall beginning to creep in. Change is in the air. There isn't much of the month left but even in the last days we still hear the Song of September.

I look forward each year to hearing the Song of September. It is the time when the seasons collide as it also is a time of great fishing. I have been listening to the Song of September for many years and hope it will play for many more.

MY LIFE WITH BOATS

The first boats I remember were in Sheboygan, Wisconsin. I was about five then. My grandparents lived there and Grandpa took me down to the harbor marina. There would be fancy cruisers and big sailboats. I loved looking across the pier to see the forest of masts swaying in the breeze. It ignited my imagination. I wanted one of those boats.

In those days in the late 1950s and early 60s commercial fishing was still a major part of Sheboygan and the fishing fleet was lined up along the Pigeon River. The area smelled of fish and I remember exploring along there, peering into the boats and seeing the nets drying on racks and all the other equipment like net floats scattered about. To me it was exciting

Sheboygan also had and still has a Coast Guard station. Once my grandfather talked a Coast Guard guy into taking us into their biggest ship and giving us a tour. I remember the engine room with gears reaching to the ceiling. I also remembered everything to include the engine room was so clean and painted. It looked like it never was used and I wondered how they could keep it that clean when they were working. I wanted someday to be on one of those boats and now looking back on my life from the vantage point of being a senior citizen I wonder, when I was young, why I didn't join the Navy or Coast Guard instead of the Army.

As soon as I started fishing my fascination with boats took another direction; towards fishing boats rather than Navy ships. By that time my family lived north of Oshkosh, half mile from Lake Winnebago. There wasn't a boat I didn't like or didn't want to own. Owning a boat was a pipedream for me in those days since my quarter a week allowance wasn't going to pay for a set of oars let alone a fishing boat.

A lot of people couldn't afford boats then. In those days, boats rentals were a fairly lucrative business. A couple of roads over from where we lived there was an old man on the lake who rented aluminum boats. My grandfather owned a small green three and a half horse power Kiekhaefer Mercury motor. My guess is his motor was manufactured shortly after the Second World War, well before the days the Kiekhaefer name was dropped and Mercury went first to white and later to black outboard motors.

During the summer when my grandparents visited meant Grandpa and I could go fishing. We drove over to the old man who rented the boats and for something like five dollars a day Grandpa rented one of his boats. He had several different varieties of boats but my favorites were Alumacraft and whenever possible Grandpa rented one of those. Grandpa hooked up his Kiekhaefer Mercury to it and put me in the boat. I drove the boat back to the bay at the end of the road my parents lived on while Grandpa drove the car over. We pulled the boat up on shore once I got there, ready to go fishing the next day. I thought I was pretty grown up when Grandpa let me drive the boat all by myself. It was just a little motor and only a couple of bays away but for a thirteen old boy it was special trust Grandpa placed in me and I was proud of it. From that time on my dream was to own an Alumacraft boat with a Mercury motor. It was the ultimate boat combination as far as I was concerned.

A couple years later Grandpa finally bought a boat and trailer. It was a wood boat with a fiberglass covering. It was a pretty boat with varnished wood on the inside. I looked at it as Grandpa's and mine. When we came back from a fishing trip it was my responsibility to sponge out any water, rubbing the sponge between the ribs to remove any moisture which could rot the wood.

Grandpa and I fished on Lake Winnebago and the Fox River in that boat. Grandpa always let me drive the boat and again I thought I was big stuff. Grandpa just pointed out across the water and I drove the boat in the direction he indicated when suddenly he yelled to stop. I turned off the motor, we dropped anchor and started to catch fish. As I look back to those days it did seem just that easy.

I wanted a boat of my very own. I dreamed about having a boat and the freedom it would give me to fish anytime I wanted. One day I was down by the lake and found an old wood boat floating in shallow water. I pulled the boat up on shore. It was too much to believe this could be my boat. I wrote down the registration numbers and called the Department of Natural Resources to find the owner. He lived on the channels going into the lake not far from where we lived. I peddled down to his house and knocked on the door. A man opened the door and I explained I found his boat. He seemed surprised, admitting he didn't know it was gone. Then he said "you want it. It's yours." I couldn't believe it. I now had my own boat.

I talked my father into taking the car down to the lake to retrieve my boat. I had big plans for that boat. Shortly after I got it home, my parents asked Grandpa to check out the boat. He reported the transom was rotted and the boat wasn't safe to use. I was hugely disappointed. My dreams crashed in on me. Eventually it was filled with sand to became a sandbox in the back yard for my little sister.

But I wasn't giving up on having my own boat and by this time I was cutting grass and making a whole five dollars a lawn. For me it was big bucks. I heard of someone living along the lake who was selling an old wood rowboat. I looked the guy up and he was asking only ten dollars for it; only two lawns worth. I could afford that but when I looked at the boat, I found a hole about the size of a fist in the bow. The hole was above the waterline so it wasn't a major problem and I rigorously checked out the rest of the boat. I read someplace where you use a knife to test the wood to make sure the wood wasn't bad. I didn't want to go through the disappointment of having a boat with rotted wood again. I went around the boat poking it with my pocket knife. My buddy who was with me said later "I thought you were going to put holes in that boat with all the poking you did with your knife."

It seemed good otherwise so I paid the ten dollars and now finally owned my very own boat. But I had to fix the hole first so I jammed a bunch of rags in the hole, covered it with wood putty, made my own fiberglass by taking more rags and glued them on the boat over the hole. For another five dollars I bought a can of marsh green paint and painted the outside of the boat. I didn't have enough money to paint the whole boat so I found a can half full of house paint left over from the last time my father repainted the house and used it for the interior. The outside was marsh green and the inside was a beige pink, the same color as the house. I borrowed oars and a life preserver from Grandpa's boat and I was all set up. The world laid in front of me.

For the next few years, I had a lot of adventures in that boat. I rowed that boat all over. I remember warm summer mornings before the sun brought on the heat of the day. The oars squeaked in the oar locks and I think most people could hear me before they saw me. I caught perch and the occasional walleye and smallmouth bass from that boat. My boyhood friend, Gary and I fished from it and later we used to row over to Garlic Island, across from his home, where we had permission to duck hunt. I always rowed and Gary sat in back with our decoys piled between us and our guns, lunches and other equipment placed in the front of the boat.

In spring during Easter break, Gary and I used my boat to again row over to Garlic Island for a couple days of camping. We sat in the boat with all of our camping gear jammed around us feeling very professional with all the gear we had and the boxes of food we raided from our parents to sustain two growing boys on such a major camping adventure. Sometime later in my teen years, I suppose about the time I discovered cars and girls, I stopped using that boat. A few years later I was married and in college when I got a call from Gary's parents. I had left the boat on shore at their boat house several years ago and they asked if they could finally get rid of it. I told them yes and although I might have abandoned my boat on shore, I still remembered all the good days from my boyhood with it.

There is one other boat from boyhood I fondly remembered. Gary's father owned an old Dunphy boat. It was made of plywood and it had a thirty-five horsepower Evinrude motor. Today it might not seem like a big motor but in its day, it was one of the best. The summer after Gary and I graduated from high school we spent a lot of time water skiing behind it. We even became good enough to ski with just one ski.

When we were a younger it was a treat when Gary's father took Gary and me fishing in the Dunphy. He motored out to a reef off the western shore in the evening and we cast for walleyes. Gary and his dad used yellow and black spinners tipped with a night crawler. I used my favorite bait in those days, the Johnson Silver Minnow. I remember the lighting strike of a fish when it hit, the coolness of the evening as the sun was sinking into the western shore, the wind dropping in the evening with the flat calm of the lake and the mad run back to their boat house just as it was getting dark.

I know some years later Gary's dad sold the boat and I hope some collector still has it. Wood boats were disappearing rapidly then as the fiberglass runabouts took over the market. Grandpa's boat and that Dunphy instilled in me a love of old wood boats and many years later as a magazine writer I found myself writing stories about them. Many of them are gone now but a few still survived either having been carefully stored over the years or refurbished and telling the stories of those old boats has become a favorite subject for me.

It was in the very early 1970s when Grandpa and I went

on our last fishing trip together in his boat. We went out on Lake Winnebago on a summer day, still cool in the early morning. We fished the old spots we fished years earlier and for the only time I can remember we did not catch fish. Perhaps it was an omen. He was getting older and I think he was losing some of his enthusiasm for fishing. Sometime shortly after that he took his boat back to Sheboygan and sold it. As I look back now, I wished I had his old green Kiekhaefer Mercury. I am sure his wood boat has long since been destroyed. Grandpa would die the next year from a heart attack triggered by shoveling snow after a blizzard. Six months later I enlisted in the Army and although I didn't know it then it was the beginning of a military career which took me to a lot of new waters.

I just returned from my first tour to Germany, now stationed at Fort Leonard Wood in Missouri. After a year in Missouri, I was leaving the Army to return to college with the expressed purpose to get my degree and a commission as a lieutenant in the Army and to return to active duty.

Just before leaving Missouri my wife and I received a tax refund check. We decided to each take a hundred dollars and buy something we wanted. She bought a sewing machine. I bought a twelve-foot aluminum jon boat. They made them in the area and I bought a brand new one for a little less than a hundred dollars. We owned a little American Motors Gremlin car and I drove back home to Wisconsin with the jon boat tied to the top of the car. I think the boat was longer than the car.

I didn't have a motor for my boat but found a Eska three and a half horse outboard with a dent in the gas tank for sale at the K-mart in Oshkosh. Although it was brand new,

I pointed out to the clerk in the sporting goods department it was damaged. He was willing to settle for seventy-five dollars and I had my first outboard motor. It was the same size motor my grandfather once had. In the next eighteen months I used it as often as I could. I took it perch fishing in Little Lake Butte des Morts and trolling for walleyes on Lake Winnebago. I also used it for duck hunting. It could easily go into shallow water and we hid the boat in the weeds and it was steady enough to shoot from. One of the things I found out about jon boats is they are very versatile boats. In Missouri we had used them to float fish rivers. When I got my commission, we headed to Alabama for officer training and then back to Germany. We needed the money for all the moving and traveling we were going to do in the next several months so my wife sold her washer and dryer, a dish washer and the sewing machine and I sold some photographic dark room equipment, an old set of skis and the boat.

Four years later we were back in Alabama and this time it was going to be for a while. I needed a boat. I was promoted to captain but with three kids' money was still tight in those days. The new bass boats coming out were out of my price range even for the used ones. I was looking through the daily newspaper and saw a classified for a jon boat with trailer selling for three hundred dollars. I could afford that. It was a fourteen-foot boat so it was a little longer than my first jon boat. I got it home and found another ad for an outboard motor for three hundred dollars. It was a seven and a half horse Eska. It looked just like my first Eska but a bit bigger. I was all set.

The next Sunday, I took it out for the first time by myself as something of a shakedown cruise. I went to one of the lakes close to home. It was a huge impoundment and with only a small motor I knew I wasn't going far. You can spend your time running around in the boat or you can fish so for the rest of the time I fished that lake I restricted myself to the first five miles of the lake. On the first day I picked up a couple of bass off rocky points and then fished an island as my last spot for the day. On two back-to-back casts I caught bass. I considered that a good omen.

I didn't even have a trolling motor yet. When I got to a spot, I wanted to fish I used a paddle to get around. It worked out nicely and I caught a bunch of fish that way. I remember leaving the landing one late afternoon as two guys came in with a fancy bass boat. I think they had more electronics on their boat than I had in my living room. They had four fish between the two of them. In the next couple of hours until dusk I fished a couple of points and then worked back into the bays, still paddling around. I caught four bass by the dusk and it was then I realized you didn't need a fancy boat with a lot of gadgets to catch fish. Eventually I did get a small transom mount trolling motor but there were times I still used the paddles.

From there we went to the Appalachian Mountains in North Carolina. There was a lot of trout fishing there so I didn't use the jon boat as much. But there were a several small ponds around so I still used the boat from time to time. There was one small lake nearby loaded with big bluegills. I could not use the outboard there but the trolling motor got me around just fine. I used a fly rod with poppers. I would the cast and holding the rod with one hand I used the other hand on the trolling motor to keep the boat in place. When a I heard a pop as a bluegill hit the popper,

I set the hook and while the fish fought against the rod, I switched off the motor so I could use both hands to bring it in. Three years later I was on my way back to Europe so I brought the jon boat back to Oshkosh, storing it and the trailer in my parents back yard. Eventually I gave the boat to one of my dad's friends but kept the motor. I still have it in my garage although I haven't used it in over twenty years.

I was back in the states four years later, this time in Minnesota and only a couple years away from retiring for the Army. I needed a different boat. I worked with a guy who had an older bass boat with a forty horse power Suzuki outboard he was selling since he was buying a new boat. I bought it. It was a low riding fiberglass boat from some of the earliest bass boat designs. My wife and I christened the boat with a can of Miller Lite beer, hooked it up to the trailer and set out for our first fishing trip in the new boat. There was some excitement when we forgot to put in the plug and I had trouble starting the engine. Both problems were my fault and when we finally got the boat back on the trailer, I realized what I had done. The motor worked fine and anyone who has owned a boat has at least once or twice forgot to put the plug in. That afternoon Becky and I caught a bunch of perch on ultralight rods with small jigs. I thought again this was a good omen.

I retired from the Army and a month later the fellow I bought the boat from retired from the Army too. We became friends after that as did our families and he and I became fishing buddies. He told me he caught a lot of bass in that boat. Becky and I would catch a lot bass in that boat too. We moved from the Twin Cities to Hudson, Wisconsin and found lots of small lakes loaded with bass in the northwest corner of the state. Our boat was just the right size for these lakes. A few years later I replaced the Suzuki with a forty horse Mercury. A year later I noticed we were getting a lot of water in the boat each time I pulled the plug when we took the boat out of water. The diagnosis wasn't good. The fiberglass on the keel was wore down to the wood frame and was leaking. It could be fixed but it was only a temporary solution. We ultimately needed to get a new boat.

Becky and I spent the winter looking at new and used boats. We decided to replace it with an aluminum boat. We went to boat shows and marine dealers and one day walked into Warner's Dock in New Richmond and there it was. It was something like love at first sight. It was a tan and green sixteen and a half foot long Alumacraft, used but only for one year. It was a transom steer boat and we asked about mounting our one-year-old Mercury motor on it with a consol steer. They could put in a consol and mount our motor, put on our old bow mounted trolling motor and switch over our depth finder. We didn't think too long about it. We said yes. There was snow on the ground when we dropped off the old boat to have the new boat rigged and ready for spring. There was a tear in Becky's eye as we drove home. Our boat was a member of the family. Then it dawned on me. I now had an Alumacraft boat with a Mercury motor. I now had the boat I wanted since I was a young boy. I took thirty years and a few other boats along the way but now had the boat of my boyhood dreams.

Over the last seventeen years I owned three Alumacraft boats with, of course, only one Mercury motor. They have been dragged all over Wisconsin, northern Minnesota and several times to Canada. I am normally on the water about a hundred days a year from the middle of March to usually Thanksgiving. I am an outdoor writer so I need to go fishing. I call it research. It makes it sound like I have a real job. I am notoriously not gentle with my boats. They take a beating but so do my trucks. The mechanics at Warner's Dock, who I call the Boat Doctor, know me well. Each spring I take my boat, trailer and motor into Warner's Dock for what I call the spring checkup.

The first Alumacraft, the tan and green one, lasted eleven years. I went through three trailers with that one. In the last season I noticed a lot of water running out when I pulled the plug. I told the Boat Doctor about it when I dropped it off for the spring checkup. A week later he called to tell me the boat was shot. I told him I never thought it possible to wear out an aluminum boat. He told me he thought so too until seeing my boat. I was in a shock and now looking for a new boat. I hadn't planned on buying a boat for a couple more years. So, the Boat Doctor told me he had a real clean used boat. It was older than my current boat but in much better shape.

It was a gray Alumacraft. They took my tan and green boat in as a trade in and transferred the Mercury motor and other electronics over to the new boat and I was back on the water by the end of March. Becky went with me to get the new boat and to say good bye to the old one. She takes owning boats seriously. It was a good boat but I missed my old one. The new boat was heavier and didn't have much of a rod locker. I got one casting rod, the paddles and the back navigation light into the locker and that was it.

Finally, after another five years my motor finally died. I was back on the Mississippi River on a cold, windy, dreary late October afternoon on my way back to the landing when I heard a pop and the motor stopped working. It sounded like a very expensive pop and I instantly knew the motor finally gave up. I was still a couple miles away from the landing. I figured I could just ride the current down to the landing, keeping the boat going in the right direction with the trolling motor. Twenty minutes later two guys in a boat came by and I flagged them down, asking for a tow. They no sooner started towing me when I looked downriver to see two huge barges working their way upriver. I said a prayer of thanks. This could have been a lot worse.

Two days later Becky and I went to see the Boat Doctor. They confirmed my initial diagnosis. The motor seized up and there was nothing they could do for it. The Boat Doctor told me he never knew anyone who could wear out an outboard motor. I had the motor for seventeen years on three different boats. I can't complain; I got my money's worth. We walked back into the show room. There was my new boat and motor. It was a black Alumacraft with a fifty horse power Mercury motor. It was the last one remaining from that year's inventory. We bought it, right then and there.

In spring I took possession of the boat and was back on the Mississippi River. It is a great boat. It has two rod lockers and lots of storage room and everything worked great on it. I don't think I ever went a full year when everything worked all the time on both my boat and trailer. I did mention I am not gentle on my boats. It is everything I ever wanted in a boat. I caught a lot of fish in it this last year. My wife caught the biggest fish to come into the boat, a fourteen-pound northern pike she caught on opening day. I caught a twenty-inch bass, still swollen with spawn. I guessed it weighed over six pounds. It was the biggest bass anyone caught last year in my boat. In late fall I caught a twenty-two-inch sauger on the Mississippi. It was the biggest sauger I have ever seen. I count these as all good omens.

This might be the last boat I own. I am now on Medicare and if this boat lasts me another dozen years, I might not be fishing a hundred days a year by then and probably will have a lot tougher time pushing it in and out of the garage. Time will tell. Until then I see a lot of lakes and a lot of fish in my future. I also finally figured out why I never joined the Navy or Coast Guard. You can't cast a crankbait or flip a plastic worm off one of those ships. Why be in a boat if you can't fish in it?

AFTER WINTER

Snow covers my front lawn but as I look outside, I see a pink flamingo poking up out of the snow. It is time to go fishing.

Before anyone thinks I have been ingesting weird chemicals or have gone completely wacky with the long winter and piles of snow around my house, let me explain. Some years back I became enthralled with those plastic pink flamingos one finds all over Florida. I thought my lawn could use one. I found one, setting it out on the front lawn. From time to time, I move it around the lawn just to amuse my neighbors who probably think I am wacky anyway.

When winter starts my pink flamingo is eventually covered by snow drifts. Once I start to see the flamingo emerge from the snow, as it begins to melt, I feel spring is on its way. Now I am seeing the back of my pink flamingo showing itself as snow starts to disappear.

For me the sight of my flamingo is a sure sign of spring and with it the beginning of open water fishing. It is a direct cause and effect relationship. Seeing the flamingo means I can get out on the Mississippi River.

About the time I saw the flamingo I get a call from my

marine dealer, Warner's Dock in New Richmond, Wisconsin. I call them The Boat Doctor because in addition to selling me my last three boats they also do all the maintenance on my boat, motor and trailer. Two weeks earlier I took my boat in for what I call its spring checkup and they just called to tell me my boat is ready to go fishing.

I already have a fishing trip planned. Walleyes and sauger should be hitting on the Mississippi River. It is time to go fishing.

Once in the garage, I charge both the starting and trolling motor batteries although they didn't need much charging since they survived the winter fairly well. I put the big thirty-pound anchor in the boat. I seldom use an anchor any other time of the year except when fishing the Mississippi River. It is the biggest anchor I can find and sometimes it isn't even enough for the strong currents in the Mississippi River, swollen with the runoff from melting snow.

Next, I load heavy clothes in my vehicle. When fishing the Mississippi River in early spring I dress as if I am going ice fishing. My fishing buddy, Dennis tells me the coldest he has ever been in his adult life was with me in the spring on the Mississippi. Sitting in an aluminum boat on frigid water as a cold wind, sometimes laced with snow and ice, blowing out of the north is as harsh as any day on the ice.

In the back of my vehicle I put insulated bibs, a Gortex jacket to wear over a down jacket, fleece pullover sweater, hooded sweatshirt, and a wax cloth Stormy Kromer hat, a pair of neoprene boots and several pairs of gloves. There are days in the spring when even all this isn't enough.

Then comes the fishing equipment. I bring up the tackle

box with the heavy jigs and sinkers I use in the spring. I seldom ever use anything lighter than an ounce since the trick is to get your bait to the bottom and keep it there despite runoff, swollen water and strong currents.

I have one spinning combo rigged with a three-way rig similar to the Wolf River Rig, except I replace the bell-shaped sinker with an ounce chartreuse jig. Another spinning rod has a three-quarter ounce fire tiger colored blade spoon and another with a chartreuse Fireball Jig by Northland. You can see a pattern here. All the baits have chartreuse. It is the one color which seems to always work in the murky water found in the Mississippi River.

I also have a couple casting rod combos with a three-foot-long leader with a hook and some chartreuse beads below a heavy bell-shaped sinker. The sinker can be as heavy as three ounces to get the bait to bottom in the worst spring current.

These are packed in the rod lockers with spare rods placed in rod racks in the garage. Then of course I check the rest of the boat, insuring I have three life vests, extra gloves and a stocking cap. In a box under the counsel, I have my camera, sun glasses and all the other odds and ends I use from day to day.

The boat is ready. So am I. It is time to go fishing.

I start to watch the weather. On the day we are going fishing the forecast calls for mild temperatures with possible rain and perhaps a bit of snow. What else would I expect? It is spring and the first fishing trip of the year on open water.

My fishing buddy Dennis Virden shows up to tell me it snowed all the way from his house in Burnsville, Minnesota to just before he crossed into Wisconsin. We attach the trailer and boat, load Dennis' clothes and our lunch in my vehicle and head south for the Mississippi River. Just as we get close to the landing a light snow begins drifting down. Skies are gray but it looks like little or no wind. It is a good feeling to see the boat slide off the trailer into the water. I have waited all winter for this day.

There doesn't seem to be a lot of boats out today. At the landing there are only eleven vehicles with boat trailers. We heard the fishing has been slow but it the first time on open water so we don't care about the reports. It is just good to be fishing.

We head upriver, towards the dam a few miles north of Red Wing, Minnesota. We find only three other boats just below the dam. As we are slowly moving toward the bank, we see one boat with three fishermen in it. One guy is fighting a fish and as we pass them one of the other fishermen leans over, grabs into the water, pulling a large brown catfish into the boat. This is a good omen.

There is a rocky island splitting the lock and dam with the lock on the Minnesota side of the river and the dam on the Wisconsin side. I slowly motor the boat close to the island on the dam side. The rollers are down on the dam and it looks like the current is not as strong as we normally see this time of year. We are in a little over twenty feet of water when I tell Dennis to drop the anchor. The boat swings around with the current and the anchor rope tightens as the anchor digs in. Snow spits from the sky.

We bait hooks and drop our baits into the water. I am using a three-way rig with an ounce jig and Dennis is using a three-quarter ounce Fireball jig with a stinger hook. Both baits easily get to the bottom and stay there.

Fifteen minutes later the boat which caught the catfish drifts by. We ask how big the catfish was and they tell us it measured thirty-five inches. We congratulate them and ask if they caught anything else. They tell us the fishing is slow and have only two fish in their livewell. One was caught in over forty feet of water and the other in over thirty feet.

The rule of thumb when fishing the river is when the water is high. fish shallow and if normal or low, fish deep. I define twenty feet of water as the dividing line between deep or shallow water. The river is now just a bit above normal so I feel we will be alright where we are and besides, over the years I have caught a lot of fish at this spot close to the bank. But talking to those guys does make me wonder if perhaps fish are in much deeper water right now.

As I am working this over in my mind, I feel a light tap and when I bring up my line, I see I lost a minnow. I might have had a light strike I tell Dennis. Ten minutes later I feel a lot stronger strike and pulling back to set the hook I feel a fish pulling away. I quickly turn the fish and a moment later lead it into the net. The fish is a walleye and it looks big enough to keep. I measure the fish and it is just over fifteen inches. On the Mississippi River walleyes have a minimum size limit of fifteen inches while sauger do not have any size restrictions. The walleye goes into the livewell. Dennis wants to take a meal of fish home with him.

Although we are fishing for walleyes and sauger you can catch just about anything in the Mississippi River. In the spring we see a lot of catfish and sturgeon. It is not uncommon to catch crappies, yellow perch, northern pike, even a muskie from time to time and over the years we have even caught a couple of brown trout. Later in April when the white bass move in it is not unusual to catch a hundred fish per boat per day.

A couple more boats show up at the dam but we don't see any fish being caught. We stop for lunch and decide after lunch we will give this spot another half hour and if we get nothing, we will move across the channel to the Wisconsin bank. We resume fishing and the next thing we notice is the boat is moving. I check to find the anchor broke loose. We find ourselves in a little over thirty feet of water when we drop the anchor again. We did say we wanted to move. We fish there for about a half hour without a strike.

Dennis pulls the anchor in as I maneuver the boat back to where we had been but this time move a little further out into a bit deeper water. We drop anchor in about twenty-seven feet of water and the current swings us back and forth from twenty-five to twenty-eight feet. The current is still not very strong.

We hear the deep guttural honking of geese and look up to see a string of Canada geese working northward against the wind. Above them is a flock of snow geese yelping. Around us we see eagles twisting and turning in the sky above us, others sitting in trees screeching at each other. I look upriver towards the dam to see an eagle set its wings, glide just above the water and pluck out a fish before it swings up, away from the water. Everything comes alive on the Mississippi River during the spring.

We notice the snow has stopped. The winds remain light. It is pleasant sitting in the boat today but Dennis and I dressed for the worst weather and are comfortable. We talk of other days on the river in the spring, recalling sitting on the water in blizzards and ice storms with line freezing in the rod guides. Today is a pleasant exception.

I feel another hard tap on my line as a fish races off. This is a bigger fish and I yell for Dennis to grab the net. It puts up a tougher battle by the time Dennis pulls the net up with the fish sagging in the mess. It is an eighteen-inch sauger, swollen with spawn already starting to leak out. I twist the hook out, slipping the fish back in the water. I feel guilty about putting the fish back but hate to kill a spawning fish in the spring although I know Dennis wants a fish fry.

We notice the wind picks up a bit but is still fairly mild and the current seems to be getting stronger.

Half an hour later another fish hits. This fish is another walleye, a bit bigger than the first one we kept so it goes into the livewell. Dennis now has enough fish for a Friday night fish fry so I feel better; no more guilt about releasing the sauger knowing we have the fish fry covered.

We discuss changing spots again but notice no one is catching any more fish than we are. We decide to stay put since we are catching some fish.

A fish surges off with my bait. This is no tentative strike. It slammed it. "Big fish," I yell to Dennis. My spinning rod is bent in half and the tip is plunging. The fish runs off and I stop it, starting to get it coming toward the boat but it keeps darting off. Slowly I get the fish closer and we can now see it. Dennis gets the net under the fish, pulling it in the boat. It is a big walleye, thick and feisty. It measures twenty-one inches. I get the hook out, taking a photo before I slip it back in the water.

As Dennis and I return to the landing we are happy. It is our first day on open water after what has been a long winter. The weather was fairly nice for this time of the year, we weren't skunked and Dennis got a fish fry. Can't ask for much more from the first fishing trip.

A SUMMER LEAVE

I had not realized until I thought about it as I was packing the car. I had not waded in a trout stream for over five years. There were reasons for that of course.

Five years earlier my father, brother David, and I fished the Woods Creek in northern Wisconsin not far from the Upper Michigan boarder. It was the last Opening Day I was in Wisconsin. We caught limits of brook trout with dark sides and orange bellies. I remembered the weekend as cloudy, chilly and damp. The evergreen trees stood out against the hard wood trees still bare and gaunt looking, waiting for spring to make them flourish. The water in the Woods Creek was not particularly high for the first weekend in May but it was higher than we would have found it in summer. The water was cold, rushing and tugging at our legs as we waded. The trout hit hard and David and I filled our limit of brook trout within a couple of hours on both Saturday and Sunday.

A week later I graduated from the University of Wisconsin-Oshkosh and that afternoon at an ROTC ceremony my father and wife pinned gold bars of a second lieutenant on the epaulets of my Army green uniform. The next day with my wife and two daughters we left Wisconsin heading south to Fort McClellan, Alabama for officer training. Six months later I would return to Wisconsin and went duck hunting one last time before leaving for a three-year tour to Germany. My son would be born there and I was promoted to first lieutenant. A few months before I left, I was selected for promotion to captain and extended my tour in Germany a couple more months before leaving to return home in time for Christmas. I would go ice fishing again. Now with my wife and three kids we headed back to Fort McClellan. I went through another Army course, made captain, and became an instructor at the Military Police School there and one day realized it had been a long time since I saw Wisconsin in the summer. Those years went by way too fast.

The course I taught had a several week break so I put in for a two week leave. We loaded the trunk with luggage, jammed the three kids into the back seat, and pointed the car north as we drove off. We barely crossed the Alabama boarder into Tennessee when the "stop poking me," started but it ended by the time we left Kentucky. It was a two-day drive and once we got around Chicago everyone was looking forward to getting out of the car.

The corn fields of Wisconsin looked wonderful. We were happy to see them and once again we were driving on Highway 41 getting closer to home with every mile. Finally, we pulled into my parent's driveway. It had been a long two days.

I think the first meal we had was bratwurst on the grill. In those days you never found good old Wisconsin bratwurst outside the upper Mid West and we missed them. Even when we were in Germany, where they have lots of various sausages they call wurst, there is nothing like bratwurst from Wisconsin. It was summer time in Wisconsin and it was hot but it was a lot milder hot than Alabama hot. After dinner Dad and I sat outside looking at the lush green woods behind my parent's home. By Alabama standards it was almost cool. Dad and I were talking fishing and we quickly planned the first fishing trip. We only had ten days before we needed to start back for Alabama.

A couple days later Dad and I were on our way to the Mecan River. It is west of Wautoma and has always been one of our favorite trout streams. Nothing seemed to have changed in the last five years as we drank coffee while driving, stopped in Wautoma for donuts, drove off Highway 21, the fields now being irrigated, getting more excited as we got closer to the stream. The car rattled over the bridge at Dakota, taking the road running parallel to the stream, and then Dad pulled the car into the high grass in the ditch next to a sandy track which led to the water. The trunk was popped open, waders pulled on, arms thrust through fishing vests, putting two-piece spinning rods together, attaching spinners to the lines and finally draping creels and nets around our necks. We followed the sandy trail through the pines. There was that smell of pines and ferns I missed and the sun light filtered through the lush woods around us. Then I saw the stream. It was a ribbon of clear water flashing through the trees. I think I finally was home.

The water felt cool against my legs as I slid down the grassy bank into the Mecan River. It felt good to feel the stream tugging at me. Dad and I went into the stream at different spots. It felt familiar yet distant to be wading the stream, working my way upstream, dropping my spinner under overhanging trees and alongside submerged logs and brush. Dad and I fished spinners. Our favorites were Rooster Tails, Panther Martins and Mepps. We used an underhanded cast to drop our baits close to cover. It had been a long time since I last fished a trout stream so I thought I would be rusty and might take some time to get the rhythm back to getting any accuracy with those casts. But I was surprised when within a few minutes it all came back to me.

Then there was that first strike of a fish hitting the spinner and the fish rocketing to the top of the water. My light spinning rod bouncing as the fish fought against it and quickly pulling the net up under the fish. It was a keeper brown trout and the first stream trout I caught in a long time. It felt good to hold that fish before slipping it into the creel.

By the time I returned to the car to meet Dad for lunch I had a half dozen trout. In those days we could keep ten trout a day as long as they were over six inches long. For lunch we had cold left over bratwurst sandwiches from the night before. We had them with mustard and onions, washed down with a cold Special Export beer, wet from the ice chest. It was Dad's favorite beer and to this day whenever I see Special Export beer I think of him.

By the end of the afternoon, I caught my limit. With the first couple of fish I caught, I wasn't very discriminating. If they were legal, they went into the creel but by the afternoon I threw back some of the smaller keepers, so I could prolong the fishing. I didn't want to catch my limit too fast and have to stop fishing. By late afternoon we met back at the car again. The fish were dumped in the ice chest on top of the ice covering the remaining two bottles of beer. After pulling off vests and waders, taking apart the spinning rods and putting them back in the trunk we had the last two beers before driving home. On the way home we had a candy bar. It was part of the tradition. I remember our favorite was a Mounds bar. On the way home I was tired but satisfied. It had been a long time since I last caught a limit of trout.

A couple days later my brother David and I fished Lake Winnebago. We fished from shore on a rocky point. We waded out into the water, wearing shorts and tennis shoes. It was early morning and a cool breeze came off the lake washing waves onto the rocks. Sunlight danced off the tops of the waves. We cast spoons. We started with flashy silver spoons and David and I caught white bass. They struck hard as they tore off, doubling over our light spinning rods. Sometimes they vaulted out of the air, splashing back into the lake. We had ten or so on a stringer within an hour.

I switched to a frog-colored spoon and after about ten or fifteen minutes I was considering switching to another spoon since I hadn't gotten a strike yet, when I felt a fish slam into my bait. I pulled back to set the hook and for a moment nothing moved. The fish burst off in a streak of speed. The drag on my spinning reel was singing as it gave out line. I finally stopped the fish, turned it but it raced off again. This happened a couple times before I started getting it closer to shore. It was just under the surface of the water and I could see it was a big northern pike. The fish pulled away but it didn't have the same strength it first had. I pulled back turning the fish again and it was coming in. Of course, we didn't have a net so I thought I would just let the waves roll it up on shore. It was close to the rocks and as I gave the final pull to beach it the spinning rod broke in half. I grabbed for the fish as it opened its mouth. I was use to lipping bass down south and forgot how sharp those pike teeth can be. But I quickly learned again as it clamped down on my thumb. I yelled as I threw the fish on the bank and looked down to see my thumb sliced open and bleeding.

It was the end of our fishing for that morning. Back at the car I wrapped my thumb in a rag and got the bleeding stopped by the time we got back home. They don't have any northern pike down south but I had caught enough of them when I lived in Wisconsin and should have known better but had momentarily forgotten. It would be a mistake I would never repeat again. With the bleeding stopped I filleted fish and we cooked them on the charcoal grill. A lot of people complain about white bass, especially in the summer, but they taste just fine when grilled.

I couldn't fish every day. There were relatives and old friends to visit and other things to do. One day we went to Milwaukee. We did some shopping, visited the zoo and took the kids to a Brewers baseball team. But ten days goes by fast and it was getting to the end of the leave. No one was looking forward to the two-day drive back to Alabama. We got used to summer not being blistering hot, knowing we would have to go back to it eventually.

It was only a couple of days left before we had to leave when Dad and I returned to the Mecan River. It was an overcast day and the day a bit cooler. As I slid into the water, I knew it was going to be awhile before I would be back again and I was relishing this last trout fishing trip. The water was a bit dirty. There had been a light rain a day or two before. I figured the fish would not be holding as tight to cover as they had earlier when it was bright and sunny. I still targeted my casts toward cover but every now and then just sent a cast across the middle of the stream, especially if there was a deep pocket.

My spinner stopped halfway across a deep pocket. It felt bigger than any of the fish I caught the other day. The fish stayed deep and made a couple short runs bucking the spinning rod in my hand. I could see the fish was a good-sized fish and was very happy once I brought it into the net. I waded to shore so there would be no chance of the fish sliding out of my hand when I put it into the creel. It was a fourteen-inch brown trout. For me it was the beginning of the day of the big trout. An hour later I caught a thirteen-inch trout.

It was getting to be late afternoon. I didn't want the day to end but I knew it was inevitable. Time was clicking down. There was a deep pool at the end of my run and I approached carefully. I looked it over for a moment and then flipped my spinner across it. I saw a flash of light in the water and then felt a jolt. I set the hook and the fish tore off. My drag even gave out a bit of line by the time I stopped the fish. It made a determined fight right in the middle of the pool staying deep. It took a couple of minutes before I was able to bring the fish to the net. It sagged in the mesh still twisting and turning as I waded for the bank. It was another fourteen inch brown.

I cleaned the fish on the bank as I was trying to savor the trip just a little longer. I looked downstream from where I came and then upstream to waters I had not fished on this trip. Maybe next time. I knew it was over for now. The fish were cleaned and in the creel. I pulled the creel out of the water with water dripping out of the bottom, started walking back through the woods toward the road. I was hoping to return soon. Perhaps next summer.

A couple days later I hugged my parents, said good bye and loaded the kids in the back seat again. In the trunk was an ice chest full of packs of frozen bratwurst. The corn fields disappeared the further we drove. It got a lot warmer the longer we drove south and then finally into our driveway and we all spilled out of the car. The next day I was returning to work. Later that evening after unloading the car and putting most everything away I called my parents to tell them we had arrived back at our home safely. No matter how old you get, your parents still worry about you. Just before we hung up my father said to me "you know Mike, maybe the fishing gods smiled down on you since you were gone so long so they gave you such good fishing." I think they did.

A WISCONSIN FISH FRY GOES TO SOUTH DAKOTA

"Here's one," I said as I pull back on my spinning rod. The rod is bent in half and the tip is plunging as a fish takes off. I turn the fish but it stays deep, running again. I stop the fish, getting it coming back toward the boat.

"Need the net?" Doug asks.

"I'm not sure," I say. "Let's see what it is first." Then we see the fish in the murky river water. It is a thin, gray shape and I yell "it's a keeper."

I hear Doug drop his spinning rod as he grabs the net. He extends the net as I lead the fish into it, pulling up underneath it. It is a fifteen-inch sauger.

"Another one for South Dakota," I tell Doug as I twist the hook out of the fish, dropping it in the livewell.

Doug Hurd, of Eagan, Minn., and I are fishing the Mississippi River at the dam north of Red Wing, Minn. It is a cool, windy day in late October. We hear the current of the river churn around us as we are anchored close to a rocky island in about twenty feet of water. Overhead we hear the shrill yelping of snow geese mixing with the deeper guttural honking of geese. Eagles soar overhead cavorting on wind currents. It is gray with the promise of rain.

We are here on a mission to get the last fish we need for a fish fry we take to South Dakota in three weeks. For a number of years, a group of four of us hunt pheasants on a farm on the very northern edge of South Dakota. We usually arrive on Thursday night and hunt Friday and Saturday. On Friday night we host the family of the farm we hunt to a Wisconsin style fish fry.

The fish are walleyes and saugers we catch in the Mississippi River. Every year Doug and I, first in the spring and later in the fall, catch enough fish for our South Dakota fish fry. It is all a part of the tradition of our hunting trip and it is a way for us to repay the family for their hospitality and making us a part of their family.

Doug sets the hook and yells "good fish." I reel my line in, grab the net and move to the back of the boat as Doug fights the fish. It makes a couple of short runs when a fat, golden brown shape of a walleye comes into view as I thrust the net in the water.

"This should make the livewell," Doug says as he measures the fish. "Sixteen inches." he tells me, dropping the fish in the livewell."

Three weeks later it is a bright sunny, very windy day in South Dakota.

Doug and I are with Howard "HoJo" Johnson and his son Nate from St. Paul. We are hunting the cattle farm of David and Dixie Melland and Dave's parents Dean and Anna Melland. Dean once introduced himself as the senior member of the firm.

It is the first afternoon of our hunt as Doug and I are walking on opposite sides of a ditch, overgrown with trees, brush and grasses. The wind always blows across the prairie but today it is exceptionally strong as it rattles the tree limbs in the ditch between us.

There is an explosion of feathers and cackles as a pheasant launches itself on Doug's side gaining height as it climbs in the air. As Doug brings his shotgun up a rooster flushes in front of me, racing along the edge of the brush. I hear Doug fire as I bring my double barrel up and fire. My bird collapses, falling into the side of the tree line.

I yell over to Doug I have a bird and he yells back he has one too. Doug walks across part of the field to where he finds his bird laying on the ground. I continue walking the outside edge of the ditch to where I saw my bird drop to find it wedged in the branches of a small tree. Reaching up, I pull it down.

"We got a double," I yell and Doug smiles as he lifts his bird up.

It is now late Friday afternoon. The western sky is yellow with slashes of pink and purple as darkness begins to creep across the prairie. It is still windy with a cold bite to it. We are in a tractor storage building. Outside Doug is cleaning birds while HoJO and Nate and I are getting the fish ready.

It will be a Friday night fish fry like the thousands of Friday night fish fries throughout Wisconsin. The fish are unthawed and we pull plastic bags of fillets out of the ice chest, lay paper toweling on a table, placing walleye and sauger fillets on the toweling and covering them with more toweling to dry them off. We fill two plastic bags with breading. The breading I use is Andy's Fish Breading I find at Fleet Farm. I buy it in the five-pound bag so it lasts me almost a year.

On the table we have about four dozen fillets. This is no small operation.

We drop five or six fillets at a time in the bags with the breading and shake the bag until the fillet is covered in breading. We place the now breaded fillets on wax paper in an aluminum pan. Each level is about ten fillets and then we place another sheet of wax paper down for the next layer of fillets.

By the time Doug finishes cleaning the birds, putting them on ice in the ice chest, all the fillets are breaded so we drive down the gravel road to David and Dixie's house. The back of the truck is filled with all the equipment we need for our fish fry.

We decide to get out of the wind by setting up on the side of the house where there isn't any wind for both our comfort and to protect the flames on the stove. The wind is still blasting across the open prairie. I have a two burner stand up Camp Chef stove we set up, hooking it to a twenty-pound tank of propane. It has a combined 60,000 BTUs when it is lit. It sounds like a jet engine taking off as we light the burners. "Satellites with thermal imaging might report a rocket has been launched from South Dakota," Doug says as there is a rush of sound and heat from the burners. Next to the cooker we set up an old card table. The aluminum pan with the fish and two more aluminum pans lined with paper toweling, we will use to dump the cooked fish, are placed on the table. Also, I set out a couple of slotted spoons, a large flashlight and a plastic bag with bottles of spices for the potatoes.

A Wisconsin fish fry could come with any number of potato options. French fries or potato salad are most common. Both of those have some problems when being transported and kept in an ice chest for a couple of days. Because of that we boil canned round potatoes. They are easy to transport and we don't have to worry about spoilage, are easy to make when cooking over a camp stove and most importantly taste good with melted butter and spices. Although perhaps not the most traditional potato for fish fries it has become part of our Wisconsin fish fry tradition we export to South Dakota.

I forgot to pack a large pot for the potatoes so we borrow one from Dixie. Hojo goes inside with a dozen cans of round potatoes where he will open the cans and dump the potatoes with the water in the pot. I pour a gallon bottle of vegetable oil into the fish fryer and it is starting to heat up.

I send Nate into the house with several bottles of tartar sauce, a loaf of dark rye bread with a quarter pound of butter to give to Dixie to put on the table. Rye bread is again one of those Wisconsin fish fry traditions. Years ago, bread was served with fish so if you got a fishbone caught in your throat, eating bread would force it down. Although that is not so much a concern today, serving bread with fish has evolved into part of the meal. It has never been any other bread such as wheat or white bread with a fish fry either. It has always been rye. I am not sure why but the taste seems to go well with fish and again it is part of the Wisconsin tradition so we follow it in South Dakota as well.

Nate takes in a large dish of coleslaw. I have never seen a fish fry in Wisconsin where you didn't get coleslaw. I admit coleslaw might be a bit of an acquired taste. As a boy, going to fish fries with my parents, I never liked the little paper cup of coleslaw sitting on the side of the plate of fish. However, as an adult I love coleslaw and eat it often with a number of other dishes besides fish. Certainly, with fish you need to have coleslaw. It is the Wisconsin way. I used to bring creamy coleslaw but now I bring vinegar coleslaw. Several years ago, my wife made vinegar coleslaw from a recipe my mother gave her. It was a hit in South Dakota and I got several compliments on it so it is only vinegar coleslaw now.

Nate and HoJo return with a large pot of potatoes, placing it on the other burner. By now the oil is bubbling and I drop in the first half dozen fillets. There is this wonderful smell of frying fish mingling with the cool night air.

It reminds me of countless fish fries I have been a part of all over Wisconsin and northern Minnesota and even in such diverse places as Panama and Spain and of course Canada. A lifetime of memories come from the fish pot as the fillets bubble and boil in oil. Doug turns on the flashlight so we can see how the fillets are coming along.

By this time David comes out with bottles of beer, handing one to me. I remark there must me a law in Wisconsin you can't fry fish without a beer. Doug who was born and raised in Wisconsin says he believes it is true.

David has just returned from doing the evening farm chores. He hunted with us most of the day but left before we made the last drive of the day.

The first fillets come out of the oil, draining the last of the oil and are dumped in one of the aluminum pans lined with paper toweling. I take one of the fillets and break it up, passing out pieces to Doug, HoJo, Nate, David and myself. This is one of the benefits of standing around the stove when the fish are being cooked. The collective opinion is the fish are good.

By now a group of barn cats surrounds around us. There seems to be about a dozen of them, crowding close to us hoping for a handout. They are an impatient group, starting to jump into the box we brought the stove in and the plastic box we stored the other cooking supplies. Some of the more energetic cats try to jump for the card table so we keep pushing them back but occasionally they are rewarded for their persistence when I throw them a small piece of fish that fell off a fillet.

Half of the fish are done and I give the aluminum pan to Nate to take inside for Dixie to put in the oven to keep warm. I drop another half a dozen fillets in the fish fryer. We have a robust fish fry for what is normally a large group. Besides the four of us hunters there are David and Dixie and their four daughters, sometimes with boyfriends in the past now two husbands. Dean and Anna will join us as well as the occasional niece or nephew. It can be a large group and that is ok. Big families are always more fun.

We are starting to get to the bottom layer of fillets. The potatoes are boiled. As the last fillets are dropped, we pour the water off the potatoes. Nate tips the big pot while I am holding the colander catching the potatoes as the water drains off. I have spent a couple minutes impressing upon Nate how important it is he does not pour any hot water on my hands. He smiles and nods he understands. I dump the potatoes back in the pot and throw in three sticks of butter to melt. I stir the potatoes and melting butter while adding a bit of garlic, a bunch of white pepper and Italian seasoning.

The last fish come off the stove and Nate takes the second

pan of fish into Dixie to put in the oven to keep warm. I turn off the burners, grabbing the pot with the potatoes and head inside. The first pan of fillets is on the stove and I put the potatoes next to it. Next to the stove is the bowl of coleslaw, a plate with the rye bread and butter and bottles of tater sauce. People are lining up to serve themselves and once filling their plates they move to the dining room table or living room where another table is set up.

As can be expected with this large family gathering there is lots of noise and it is a good thing. There are stories of the days hunting, jokes and laughter and more stories of farming and family life. I sit next to Dean and he tells me of the days he was boy riding a horse to a one room school. Although now abandoned, the school house still stands and we have hunted near it, peering in the door to see the old student desks.

Some are going back to the kitchen for seconds on fish. It is a huge compliment. Outside it is still windy and temperatures are dropping. It could snow as it has in other years. The fish fry with fish caught in Wisconsin and cooked like it is in Wisconsin is a success. But the success comes because of the people. A fish fry or any dinner is as much about those you are with as it is the food.

MY PLAYGROUND

I grew up in the country a few miles north of Oshkosh, Wisconsin. We lived a half mile from Lake Winnebago and all around me were woods and fields. It was my playground and a great place to be a kid.

My playground started right out my back door with the woods in back of our house. It was there I learned to walk in the woods. Even before I was old enough to have a shotgun, I spent hours in the woods throughout the year. I enjoyed every season in the woods and got to know it like the back of my hand.

It wasn't that big but it seemed big enough for me. A few deer were seen in the woods from time to time. It still was worth calling the entire family to the windows in the back of the house when we saw deer at the edge of the woods or in our back yard. My father had a large garden in our back yard but he never minded when the occasional deer stopped by for a snack. I guess he figured there was enough there for everybody. Deer were never hunted in our area. Deer Hunting was an "up north" activity in those days.

Later as I began hunting, the woods were my private

hunting area because no one else ever hunted there. I shot a lot of rabbits and the occasional pheasant back there. There were squirrels in the woods but it never seemed like there were that many and for some reason I never got into squirrel hunting so they had nothing to fear from me.

Around the woods there were a number of a fields with either corn or soybeans in them. I never hunted them because even as a young hunter I realized one person hunting a large field was never going to be successful. There was just too much room for pheasants to run around you. However, there was a drainage ditch running between two fields and it was just the right size for one hunter to work by himself. I always made an effort to hunt it and although it didn't happen often, every now and then I would kick out a pheasant.

Today my woods have grown larger. A couple of fields once farmed when I was a kid have been left undisturbed, now overgrown with brush. In time the brush might grow into full sized trees. Although deer were never seriously hunted in our area when I was a kid the deer population has increased and one of my mother's neighbors now bow hunts in the woods behind her house for deer and also for turkeys. We never heard of turkeys when I was a boy. They were imported sometime in the late 1960s and early 70s. Now they are everywhere. It is a great conservation success story.

There were a couple other woods all within reasonable hiking distance and I would hunt them too. These other woods had rabbits in them but it seemed not as many as the woods just behind our house. But I always hunted them anyway just to have a different place to hunt.

When I go back there now, homes are built in those

other woods or so close to them it would be impracticable to hunt there anymore. As I drive by them, I say to myself "I used to hunt rabbits there."

Also west of my parent's house was a railroad track line. When I was growing up no one seemed to mind if we hunted there. When the pheasant season began there was always the possibility of kicking out a rooster or two. Once the snow was on the ground you could find rabbits there. It was a great little hunting spot and for the most part I had it all to myself, especially in the winter.

As a kid I remember the railroad tracks as being fairly busy. I can remember, for some reason, us kids thought it fun to put a penny on the tracks so the train would squash it as it ran over it. We carried around the flattened pennies as if they were trophies. Apparently in later years, it was frowned upon people hunting the railroad tracks. Today there is one track line still there and I suppose occasionally it is still used although I do not think I have seen a train on it for years. I can't tell you when was the last time I had to wait at the crossing for a train to come by. The other track has been pulled up and is now a path for bicycles, snowmobiles and ATVs to use. I suppose kids don't put pennies on the tracks anymore either.

A quarter mile east of my parent's home is Lake Winnebago. The road running past our home ended at the lake. Some people used it as a boat landing and for a number of years you would normally see cars with boat trailers parked there. A grassy area just to the south of it was part of our playground too.

There also was a sandy beach and we kids swam there as often as our parents would let us. Right after school let out, we wanted to go swimming but our parents told us the water was too cold. To kids, who want to go swimming, no water is too cold so we could not understand our parent's restrictions. However, usually within a couple of weeks we were allowed to finally go swimming, in part I suppose to finally stop us from whining why we couldn't go swimming. For several years, I think I spent just about every day during summer vacation swimming there.

Our swimming hole came to an end as did the boat landing. People from the city began to move out there and they built homes on the grassy field. They didn't like people using the end of the road as a boat landing and discouraged us kids from swimming in front of their homes. There was some yelling and screaming as I remember and we kids resented these people for taking away our swimming area.

But there was one area just east of the homes on the lake that wasn't touched. It was a wooded area bordering the rocky shore right to the water. I began to explore it and the people who lived in the houses closer to the road never bothered me when I was there.

Again, it was another private playground. For some reason and I'm not sure why, there seemed to be a slightly mysterious and spooky element to this area. No one except me ever seemed to venture into it. I felt it too but it could have been my overly active imagination at work. It didn't stop me; it just added to the adventure. I found a small tar paper shack in the woods. It was probably about the size of an ice house and may have once been one, abandoned there some many years ago. It was part of the mystery.

Another time in the fall, I was exploring these woods and found a wooden decoy washed up on the rocks. It was bit battered and some of the paint was worn off but otherwise in fairly good condition. I kept it. I did some research on it and think it is a Mason decoy which is fairly prized today by collectors. Even then, back in the 1960s, I wondered why anyone would have been using these decoys, risking the chance at losing them. I still have the decoy today and it was the beginning of a small collection of twenty some wood and cork decoys now displayed in my office.

There was a small rocky point extending about six feet into the lake. As I look back at it now, I wonder if someone years ago made the point by piling rocks there. Maybe the same person who had the little tar paper shack? Throughout my youth I was a big reader of outdoor magazines and somewhere I read minnows came into the shallows in the evening and of course the bigger game fish followed them. So, one night, all by myself, I decided to test out this theory by fishing at the little point. I rode down to the woods on my bike, hid it in the woods and taking my spinning rod, waders, a small trout net, a flashlight and a couple Johnson Silver Minnows I walked through the woods to the point.

After pulling on my waders, I waded out to my thighs and started casting. I choose the Johnson Silver Minnow not only because it was my favorite artificial bait in those days but also because in front of me were weeds and again, I read fish liked to hide in the weeds. I must have been casting for about half an hour when suddenly my bait jolted to a stop. My spinning rod was doubled over and I could feel a fish thumping against it. It put up a great fight and I really wanted it. A moment or two later I was leading the fish into the net. I was overjoyed. It was a smallmouth bass and I quickly put the fish on a stringer which I tied it to a rock.

I waded back out and a few minutes later caught another smallmouth. That also went on the stringer. It was starting to get dark as nightfall descended but I kept fishing. Another fish slammed my bait. That one was a white bass. A few minutes later I had another fish on but lost it right in front of me. I wasn't disappointed. I had three fish on my stringer so it had been an extremely successful night.

Now it was dark and I waded back to shore, turned on the flashlight, tugged off my waders, slipped back on my shoes and with the flashlight I walked back out of the woods to my bike. If the woods were a bit spooky in daylight, they were a whole lot spookier in the darkness. I was very glad when I finally got my bike and started to peddle home. I felt triumphant. Not only did I find this new spot all by myself and there were fish there but I also confronted the spooky woods.

I never told anyone except my buddy, Gary, about the spot. He and I returned at least once a week through the summers to this little hot spot. Sometimes we got skunked but it didn't seem often and we caught a variety of fish. There were smallmouth bass and white bass I found the first time I fished there but also northern pike and walleyes. We never caught a lot of fish at any given time but we generally caught a couple and for young boys that was enough. The woods remained spooky at night but it never prevented us from fishing there.

Today those woods along the lake have houses built where I once explored the spooky woods. There is a road built there and now the rocky shore I once had to myself have docks jutting out in the lake. I wonder if anyone has ever thought about casting a Johnson Silver Minnow from those docks to see if there are any fish there.

The other huge part of my playground was the channels. When we first moved out to the country the channel was one huge trench leading out to the lake. Along the first part of the channel, there were a number of boat houses and closer to the lake were a couple of homes. Across the channel and behind it was a large marsh. Within a few years, several more trenches were dug out into the marsh. Even as a kid, I could recognize someone had a plan for them but throughout my boyhood they just looked like muddy ditches. There wasn't any development going on so perhaps the person who started it just ran out of money or interest in the project. That was perfectly ok by me.

It became a perfect fishing spot. I started fishing there for bullheads. Although a lot of people might not care for bullheads, I have always had a soft spot in my heart for them. I learned to become a fisherman on bullheads. They actually put up a fairly good fight, especially on the light fiberglass rod and Johnson Century reel I had then. For a second rod I had a long stick with some line tied to it. I just threw out the line on the sick so it sunk to the bottom with a small sinker and I put a bobber on the line with the spincasting outfit. If the fish were on the bottom close to the bank, I caught them with the stick and if there were off the bank, I got them on the bobber.

In the spring the crappies came into the channels and the crappie run seemed to be the highlight of spring and early summer. The run would start somewhere in early May and run for about three or four weeks. One of my neighbors was a big fly fishing guy and he would be down there catching crappies on flies. So, I went out and with my meager allowance I saved up enough to buy a cheap bamboo fly rod. The first time I tried it on crappies I actually did catch a crappie but wasn't sure how to pull the fish in so I lost it. It was a bitter disappointment for a young fisherman.

I eventually learned how to use a fly rod but discovered what I thought was a new bait. I caught my first crappie on a royal coachman fly and after that it became my favorite fly. I still use it today for panfish. However, if I was going to fish a fly with my spincasting combo I needed to get enough weight on it to cast so I added a split shot just above the fly. Suddenly I was catching bunches of crappies. What I didn't realize then was basically I had the equivalent of what would be a jig. For years the royal coachman fly with a split shot was my main crappie bait.

There were other fish in the channel besides crappies and bullheads. All of the different panfish were there as well as small northerns and the occasional bass. Some ten years later I was fishing the channels for crappies but before I started crappie fishing, I would make half a dozen to ten casts with a heavier rod and big spoon. Several times I had a hard, jolting strike but I never was able to land the fish. My guess it probably was a big northern pike.

One of the best fish I ever caught in the channels was after several days of rain. The channels were especially muddy then but I went down there anyway. I was casting a yellow and silver spinner. I now had a larger spinning rod with a Mitchell 300 spinning reel. I had come up in the fishing world. One of my buddies always had luck fishing spinners with a nightcrawler wrapped around the treble hooks. Considering how muddy the channels were, I thought the night crawler would help.

I was casting for about twenty minutes when something slammed into my bait., I pulled back and my spinning rod was bent in half and it felt for a moment as if I was snagged. Then the fish charged off. My drag let out line. Up until that time I never caught a fish big enough to take out line on my drag. This was getting exciting. I stopped the run and got the fish coming back but again it ran off. I really, really, really wanted this fish and I think I was even praying for divine assistance. The fish rolled on the top of the water making a wash tub size swirl.

This was the fish of a lifetime for a fourteen-year-old boy. I wondered what kind of fish I had. Again, it made a couple more runs before I finally got it to the bank. I looked down and it was a big catfish. It didn't matter to me. It was big fish and was all that mattered. Now I had the problem of how to land it. I didn't have a net and I am not so sure I could have gotten down to it to use a net if I did have one. I solved the problem by just dragging the fish up the bank and my line held. I was praying it wasn't going to break. Once I got it close enough, I just pounced on it. It was a channel catfish, probably weighing about five or six pounds and one of the biggest fish I ever caught at that time in my life.

A few years later there was some movement to develop the channels after being neglected for so many years. A couple of bridges were put in and roads built but nothing much more then that by the time I joined the Army in the early 1970s. But soon thereafter homes started to pop up there. Now the channels are all built up with houses and docks out front with boats tied up to them.

Change is inevitable and so it came to my playground. Some of it remains. The woods behind my parent's house is still there and intact. My father passed away fourteen years ago and last year my mother sold the house she and my father built in 1958 when she moved to an independent living apartment in town. It was another change. But what hasn't changed are the memories and I will have them always. It was a great time and place to grow up.

SMALLIES: THE MAGNIFICENT OBSESSION

The sun dances off the waters of Chequamegon Bay as a light wind ruffles the surface of the water. Oak Point stretches out in front of us. It is a line of dark green trees and rocks which have survived for thousands of years, battered by the winds coming off Lake Superior. In the shallow water are perhaps hundreds of old logs washed up against the point. Those logs broke free from the log rafts floated across Lake Superior over the last hundred years in the days of the logging boom. Today they provide cover for the huge smallmouth bass cruising these waters.

Although calm today, you can see this land and water have endured great storms and wild weather. Only the toughest live here and smallmouth bass are one of the toughest fish in these waters. Doug Hurd of Eagan, Minnesota, and I are here in search of the great smallmouth bass fishing.

It is a warm mid-June morning. Doug is slowly motoring through the water with his eyes on the depth finder.

"There is a rocky ledge right in front of us," he tells me.

"The water drops into about five to seven feet of water right off the ledge and I think this might be the best spot."

Doug pulls back on the throttle to shut off the motor, stopping us about twenty feet from the edge of the shallow water rocks. We are fishing sinking worms rigged Texas style. We cast into the edge, letting our plastic worms drop into deeper water. Within the first half dozen casts Doug pulls back, setting the hook as his rod tip plunges. A fish swirls on the top of the water before it dives and charges off.

"It's a good fish," Doug says as I quickly reel in my line, dropping the rod on the floor of the boat to grab the net. The fish makes a couple of runs by the time Doug gets it close to the boat. As I extend the net, the fish keeps darting off. Smallmouth bass are tough fish. There is no give up in them. I get the net under the fish and pull up. The fish is twisting and turning in the net as I bring it in the boat. It is a thick, muscular seventeen-inch smallmouth bass. We take a quick photo before Doug slips in back into the water.

"What a pig," Doug says as the fish bolts off.

A few minutes later Doug connects on another fish. It is about fifteen inches long. It puts up a strong, tenacious battle; never giving up. On the next cast, just after Doug releases his fish, I feel my line shooting out. I pull back on my spinning rod out of instinct. There probably is no reason for me to set the hook as the fish is on solid.

I see my line slicing through the water as the fish is racing for the surface. I am cranking furiously on my reel to get in the slack before the fish gets to the surface. I don't make it. The fish vaults out of the water, clearing the surface by about two feet before it splashes back in the water. I am lucky. The hook held and I still have the fish. My drag is clicking as it is letting out line.

Doug is now standing at the side of the boat with the net as my fish continues to race off. I turn it but the fish still doesn't give up and races off again. My spinning rod is bent in half. I start getting the fish closer but like all smallies it doesn't give up; even when I finally get the fish close enough for Doug to net it. When I press the fish against the measuring tape on the side of the boat, the fish measures seventeen inches.

"This is what we came for," Doug exclaims as I release the fish and he and I exchange hi fives.

We continue to work along the ledge and within an hour we catch nine smallmouth bass measuring from fourteen to nineteen inches. The sun is higher now in a cloudless pale blue sky when the fish stop hitting. We move into shallow water and try again without getting a strike. We try deeper water and again get nothing.

We look around us, seeing a rocky windswept point jutting out into the water, separating Chequamegon Bay from Lake Superior. At the tip of the point is a lighthouse, standing as a lone sentinel against the waves and winds which tear at it. We motor over. A rocky point with deeper water nearby should be a magnate for fish. Doug and I work it hard but do not get a strike. For the rest of the day, we hunt smallies but do not find them.

We have a broasted chicken dinner at a little restaurant in Ashland and are now back in our motel room talking and planning strategy. Out of the window in our room we see the sun sinking into Lake Superior to the west. Doug and I have been coming to Ashland and Chequamegon Bay early in the season for several years. We have been coming here because of our obsession for smallmouth bass. They are probably, pound for pound the toughest fighting fish in fresh water. In the early season, these smallies are in Chequamegon Bay in astounding numbers. We normally catch fifty or so fish a day. There are also lots of big fish. One year Doug and I both caught our personal best smallmouth bass of twenty-one inches within an hour of each other.

But this year we are stumped. We fished all the same places we caught fish in other years. We caught only nine fish and never had another strike. What has changed?

"I think we came too late this year," I suggest. Doug agrees with me. Normally we fish here mid to end of May. Even in nasty weather the smallies are hitting that time of the season. This year is different. Due to scheduling conflicts, we ended up in Chequamegon Bay in mid-June. As well, summer came early this year and temperatures are considerably warmer than expected. Doug and I fished all day in shirt sleeves. Normally we have several layers of clothing on.

"We are probably a couple of weeks late," Doug added. It was one of those things which couldn't be avoided but what do we do now? Chequamegon Bay wasn't working. Would going out on the bay another day be just another exercise in frustration? There was no indication anything was going to change for the better. Plus, we made a lengthy drive to get here. Have we wasted our time?

Perhaps not. "I have an idea," I said. "Why don't we go to Shell Lake."

"I was just thinking about that too," Doug adds.

Shell Lake is about an hour and a half drive south of

Ashland. We drove right by it on our way to Chequamegon Bay. But most importantly, Shell Lake has smallmouth bass in it. When you are obsessed with fishing for smallies it seems like a good alternative, especially when the first spot is not working out.

Doug and I are obsessed with fishing for smallmouth bass. We have been chasing them for years. For us they are hard fighting fishing, tough and tenacious. Adding to their mystic for us is you don't find them all over. For the most part, you find them in lakes in the northern third of Wisconsin or in rivers. It is a magnetic combination which fuels a magnificent obsession.

Doug and I have fished Shell Lake for a lot longer than we have been coming to Chequamegon. It was one of our first smallmouth bass haunts and we make several trips a year to it. Admittedly, the smallies there are not as big as the ones in Cheguamegon Bay but regardless of size, smallmouth bass are always fun to catch.

"Let's do it," Doug said. We walk over to the motel office to tell the folks there we are checking out the next morning and want an early wake up call.

The next morning, we stop at one of our favorite cafes in Spooner, had country fried steak and eggs with a pile of hash brown and by late morning are motoring across Shell Lake. The sun is bright, the sky is light blue with a ribbon of thin white clouds and there is only a little wind to ripple the clear water.

On Shell Lake I switch from a sinking worm to a tube jig. For years I have used only tube jigs when I fish Shell Lake. We are fishing a rocky point and I feel my jig bounce off the rocks on bottom. Suddenly I feel weight. Dropping the rod tip, I reel up the slack and pull up the rod tip. I still feel weight and now a slight thumping so I pull back hard to set the hook. My spinning rod is bouncing as the fish is racing off and then for the surface as I am trying to get the slack out of the line but the fish flips out of the water, throwing the hook.

I always hate to lose the first fish of the day. It seems like a bad omen. I think I said some unkind words. Half a dozen casts later I again feel weight. The fish is one solidly and after a brief, hard fought fight I lead the fish into the net. It is a foot long smallmouth bass. It is good start to the day and I think I shook off losing the first fish of the day.

From there Doug and I work along the shoreline. We skip tube jigs under and around docks and catch smallies. We expected that with the docks providing shade and cover on a bright sunny day. What we didn't expect was picking up fish between the docks where the fish are in the open in clear water on a sunny day.

The water in Shell Lake is amazing clear which what makes it such a special lake. Even in mid-summer, when other lakes are discolored from summer weed bloom, Shell Lake is always clear. There have been times we are sitting in ten to twelve feet of water and can see the bottom. In the clear water I have seen schools of smallmouth bass and when I cast to them, I am often rewarded by seeing a fish move towards my bait.

Today the fish appeared to be in the shallows and might be in their post spawn patterns. Sometimes we move into deeper water and still find fish. It seems where ever we go we find fish. Most of our fish are smallies but occasionally one of us picks up a largemouth bass. I am not sure if this is a good sign or not. I heard once largemouth bass become established in smallmouth lakes they take over and push out the smallies.

I would hate to see this will happened in Shell Lake since it has such good smallmouth bass fishing. Where else would Doug and I go to indulge our smallmouth bass obsession?

We are now in a spot where the shallow sandy bottom drops off into deeper water. Although it is some distance from the bank there are several boat lifts here. The owners of these boats either have long docks to get out this far or they need to wade out to get to their boats. Doug flips his bait to one side of a lift and I flip my bait to the other side.

"Got one," Doug says. I look over toward Doug and I see his spinning rod bent in half.

I feel a tick on my line and then a couple more. I strike back as an instant reaction without looking at my line. I feel a fish surge off.

I got one too," I yell as I am trying to turn the fish. The fish stops and I start getting it coming toward the boat when it takes off again. Another typical fight from a smallie. The fish dove, flew out of the water and took off again. I get it next to the boat and reaching over I grab my fish, pulling it in the boat. I look over at Doug and he is also holding his fish. Both fish look to be over a foot in length.

"A double," he says as he holds up his other hand for a high five.

"Can't ask for more," I reply as we exchange high fives.

It is late in the afternoon. We are hot and sweaty and caught a bunch of smallmouth bass. Our biggest was about sixteen inches which would have been considered an average fish in Cheguamegon Bay but it didn't matter. What started out slow in one place, ended well in another. Plus, we caught a bunch smallies. What a magnificent obsession.

CATCHING A FRIEND FOR LIFE

People come and go throughout one's life but some people become a part of your life, staying in your heart forever. One of those is my German fishing buddy, Arnold.

It's been over twenty years since the first time we met. I was invited with a group to go to the Boundary Waters in northern Minnesota. I retired from the Army a year earlier and involved in a business which wasn't doing too good so the invitation came at a good time. I needed to get away for a few days and go fishing.

A couple years earlier I put together a trip to the Boundary Waters for the Combat Support Division at the Readiness Group at Fort Snelling, Minnesota, where I was assigned. We were active-duty soldiers advising Reserve and National Guard units in Minnesota and Iowa. The trip had been a great time and was remembered fondly by those who went. A newly assigned Captain Ken Leners, who worked with me, decided to carry on the tradition after I left. Perhaps because I organized the first trip, Ken decided to ask me to return. Several members of this new group going on this canoeing trip were still in the military.

Ken also asked his father Mike Leners who lived in Iowa to join us as well as his old German landlord, Arnold Walther. When Ken was assigned to Germany as a new lieutenant he rented an apartment from Arnold.

It was when we all got together the first morning just prior to departure for the Boundary Waters when I met Arnold. Arnold would have been in his late sixties at the time and I was amazed he was willing to go on such a rigorous trip. But Arnold thrived on it. He slept on the ground, paddled a canoe all day and dragged gear over portages with relish. He became part of the group and would return over the years for several more trips. He loved the Boundary Waters and the rugged adventures we had.

I have two distinct memories of that first trip to the Boundary Waters with Arnold. One afternoon Ken and I were fishing on one side of the lake and Ken's dad, Mike and Arnold were in a canoe on the other side of the lake. We looked over to see the canoe turned over, floating on the surface of the lake. We dropped our fishing rods and started paddling furiously to get to them. The more we paddled the more concerned we were becoming but once we got closer, we saw both Mike and Arnold in life jackets swimming for shore. Although they lost all their fishing equipment, they had a great story to tell everyone that night around the campfire.

The second memory is how I became the camp cook. The original plan was everyone brought and prepared their own food. Before we left, I told Ken I would clean all the fish, keeping them on ice for a big fish fry I would put together our last evening in the Boundary Waters. One late afternoon Ken, his dad Mike, Arnold and I are sitting around a campfire making an early dinner before we went fishing to catch the evening bite. I was cooking a steak while Ken was cutting up a couple cans of Spam for their dinner. Arnold looked over at my steak, saying "It looks delicious."

I felt guilty about that and at the end of the trip I told Ken for future trips I would take care of all the cooking. I would get all the food, make a big breakfast in the morning and later when we all got back to camp make dinner for everyone. All I asked is everyone chip in for the food and if I was going to do the cooking and clean all the fish someone else take care of cleaning the pots and pans. It's a deal I was told. From then on, I became the camp cook which included not only the Boundary Waters but trips we took to Canada, South Dakota, northern Minnesota, or where ever our adventures took us. To this day I still am the camp cook.

Eventually Arnold came to stay with my wife and I. We would fish the lakes in northwestern Wisconsin were we live, before and after our other trips to the Boundary Waters or Canada. Arnold became part of our family, going with us to visit a newly born granddaughter and joining the family in baptizing another granddaughter. We also became part of his family, visiting him, his wife, Christa, daughter Kerstin and husband Daniele and granddaughter Katharina when we were in Europe.

One year he and his family came to visit us and we spent a week at a cabin on Gunflint Lake on the Minnesota/Canadian border. Arnold and Christa were celebrating their fiftieth wedding anniversary. It was a wonderful week. We listen to the haunting call of loons on the water as we made breakfasts on the deck of the cabin. Arnold and I with his granddaughter fished for smallmouth bass during the day.

We watched the sun sink behind us, disappearing in the vast dark forest of pines surrounding us.

Before and after our trip to Gunflint Lake we took his granddaughter fishing with us for panfish in one of our local lakes. Both Arnold and I enjoyed watching the thrill and excitement Katharina had as she reeled in another bluegill splashing on the surface. I took a photo of her one day, fishing cap sitting on her head and holding a big bluegill she caught. That picture still sits in a frame in Arnold's office at home in France.

Arnold also is one of only four fishermen who caught two fish on one bait in my boat. It was early evening and we were fishing crankbaits, flipping them against a rocky shoreline. Arnold yelled he had a fish and a moment or two later when he pulled it in there was a bass on both sets of treble hooks. It was quite an achievement. My wife, another young fishing buddy and I are the only other ones in my boat to catch two fish on one bait in the twenty plus years we have fished in northwestern Wisconsin.

Arnold fell in love with Wisconsin. Perhaps because so many of his country men came here in the late 1800s and early 1900s, Arnold saw the very same things which made them make Wisconsin their home. Arnold had his favorite lakes. One in particular, Squaw Lake, not far my home became special to him. He and I caught a lot of bass from that lake. There was a small island near the landing and we always made sure we fished it just before we left at the end of the day. I remember Arnold setting the hook and the water exploding as a bass raced off. Arnold's spinning rod was bent in half as the fish fought back and then finally Arnold got the fish alongside the boat, hauling the fish in. Most of the fish we caught off the island were between two and three pounds and I always expected Arnold was going to break a rod as he hoisted those fish out of the water, dragging them into the boat but he never did. A smile spread across his face as he pulled in those fish.

Arnold also became a Packer fan. Generally, he visited us in August, during the time the Packers were playing their preseason exhibition games. He watched them with us, cheering each time the Packers scored. I gave him a t-shirt with a Packer helmet on the front, advertising Old Style Beer. It became his lucky fishing shirt. In Germany he continued to follow the Packers and rooted for them throughout the season and playoffs. He was just as excited as we were when the Packers won Super Bowl XLV.

We once fished for salmon in Lake Michigan. Arnold caught the first fish, a ten-pound king salmon, later telling me it was the biggest fish he ever caught. It was a rough day with waves washing over the breakwater at Algoma. After Arnold caught his fish, he became sea sick and spent the rest of the trip laying down. By the time we got back to the harbor after dark his voice was raspy and all he wanted to do was lie down. I took him back to the room and got him in bed. "What have I done to him," I thought. I was sick with worry. Once I got him in bed, I left with the rest of the party for dinner, getting a bowl of chicken soup to take back to him. When I came back, I woke him and forced him to drink the soup. It worked. The next morning Arnold was back to his old self and I breathed a sigh of relief.

Another time Arnold visited us he was complaining about pain in his leg. We thought initially it might be just a cramp from sitting for several hours in a plane. But after a couple days when the pain didn't go away, I took him to the doctor. He had a blood clot in his leg. This could become serious. I took Arnold in for blood tests every other day. He could not fly home yet so he missed his flight back to Germany. Eventually the doctor said there was no reason he couldn't go fishing so Arnold and I went fishing until the doctor finally cleared him to travel. The Olympics were on so Arnold and I also watched the Olympics when we weren't fishing. Arnold stayed with us for another week which was ok. We got to watch the Olympics and catch more fish together.

We fished together for years and then for a number of reasons I no longer remember Arnold missed a few summers. Then it became more difficult for him to travel. It must have been disappointing to him. He traveled the world from China to the United States and now it became too much for him. Changes came to his family as well. His daughter and granddaughter moved from Germany to Switzerland for Kerstin's job in the banking industry. Arnold and his wife Christa sold their home in Germany and moved to Switzerland to be near their daughter and granddaughter. A few years later Kerstin married a wonderful man named Daniele and eventually left the bank she worked at to buy a villa in southern France, running it as a bed and breakfast. Arnold and Christa followed them to France.

We invited Arnold to visit us and go fishing again but this time it was finale. He could not travel that far again. It made us both sad. It seemed an era in our life had come to an end too. It wasn't Christmas yet and one night my wife Becky and I were sitting around the dining room table, talking while having a cocktail. We realized as we talked, if we wanted to see Arnold and Christa again, we would have to go to France. We contacted Kerstin. Yes, we should come, we were told. We started making plans and four months later in the end of March we were on a plane flying to France. We landed in Paris and the next day took a train for southern France. Arnold, Christa and Kerstin were waiting for us when we stepped off the train.

Arnold and Christa might have been a few years older than they were the last time we saw them but they didn't look any older. We all hugged and there probably was a tear or two shed. Arnold and I, two fishing buddies, were together again. That night we ate a wonderful meal of chicken salad at Kerstin's villa and Arnold and I drank a bit of bourbon like we had many nights sitting at our dining room table. Before we left for France, Becky and Kerstin exchanged a series of emails. Would it be possible for two old fishing buddies be able to fish again when we were in France? Kerstin said it could be done.

The next day Arnold, Christa, Becky and I met a guide named Joergen who took us on a tour of Provence. We saw the very spot where Vincent Van Gogh stood, painting his masterpiece Starry Night. We saw a Roman gate to a village which was a thousand years old. We ate mussels at a café sitting outside where it was warm, shaded with ancient trees. We stopped at a winery and olive plantation to taste wine and olive oil. The next day Arnold and Christa took us for a picnic along a trout stream running through their town. The water was cold and clear and in addition to trout the stream also had grayling.

A day later Arnold, Christa, Becky and I crowded once more into Joergen's car. We were on our way to the

Mediterranean Sea. Arnold and I were going fishing again. We drove to the town of Cassis. Becky and Christa went in search of places to shop. Arnold, Joergen and I walked down to the port. We found our boat. It was a commercial fishing boat which also took out sport fishermen in the afternoon. It was a bright day with sunlight dancing on the lightly rippled water, bouncing off the rocky cliffs along the sea. As the boat headed out to sea, Arnold and I looked at each other. We were smiling. We were going fishing together again.

The captain pulled the boat close to a large gray cliff and dropped anchor. He showed us how to bait our hooks with what looked like sandworms. He told us we probably weren't going to catch many big fish but we would catch fish. It was good enough for Arnold and me. Arnold caught the first fish. It was about six inches long and brightly colored. I have no idea what kind of fish it was but the captain seemed to be happy with it and had Arnold throw it in a bucket.

A few minutes later I felt a pop on my line and my light spinning rod bounced as the fish raced off. It put up a surprisingly stiff fight by the time I got it in. It was about the same size and color as Arnold's fish. A little while later Joergen caught the biggest fish, probably about a foot long. We continued to feel fish hit our baits an brought our fish into the boat, starting to fill the bucket.

The fish might not have been as big as the bass Arnold and I caught in our lakes in western Wisconsin or the walleyes we took in the Boundary Waters or the northern pike we found in Canada but we caught fish and enjoyed being on the water together one more time. The Mediterranean became just another fishing spot for us. It was a grand afternoon. When we returned to port Joergen took the fish, later making them in a soup which turned out well he said. The Mediterranean might have been different than the lakes we had fish before and fish soup is certainly different than the way we cooked fish on our other adventures together but we caught fish and had fun which is what fishing is all about anyway. Fishing trips in other parts of the world can be different but are still similar in so many ways.

Back at port Arnold, Joergen and I found a sunny café on the edge of the water and ordered a beer. Shortly thereafter Christa and Becky joined us. We touched glasses, making a toast to fishing buddies being together again.

It may have been a few years ago we last were together but at that moment it seemed like just yesterday. Joergen now became another fishing buddy too.

You can never have too many fishing buddies. Fishing is more than just catching fish. As we drank our beers, sweaty with condensation while sitting in the sun on the shores of the Mediterranean we knew it was more about the people we are with then the fish we caught. Once more, fishing buddies a world apart are together again; which is the only thing which truly mattered.

A SMELT FRY STILL BRINGING PEOPLE TOGETHER

One of the earliest signs of spring, when I was growing up in the 1950s and 60s, was the legendary smelt runs on Lake Michigan and with it the ever popular smelt fries. Every church, bar, VFW Hall and American Legion Post seemed to have them.

Eventually the smelt runs diminished and with it the smelt fries, but today in the northwestern side of Wisconsin, The Baldwin Volunteer Fire and Rescue Station has kept the tradition of the spring smelt fry alive. On the last Friday in April, they put on a day long smelt fry attracting people from all over western Wisconsin and eastern Minnesota.

Way before the famous trout and salmon fishing, we have today in the Great Lakes, Lake Michigan and Lake Superior had a thriving native trout population and with-it world renown fishing but the sea lamprey decimated the trout in the early 1950s. Smelt had been the primary forage fish for the trout and with the trout gone smelt populations exploded. In spring they came into shallow waters in such incredible numbers to spawn, making the smelt run the most exciting party to hit the beaches of Lake Michigan.

From Milwaukee to Door County, once the word got out the smelt run was on, people from all over the Mid West flocked to Lake Michigan.

Although I suppose the smelt were active during the day, it seemed most of the smelt were caught at night or at least that was when the party started.

On the beaches you would see bonfires lighting the beaches. Some people were wading in the water, netting smelt. Others stood around the fire, warming the outside from the heat of the fire and the inside with adult beverages. There was always a case a beer around. No need it keep it on ice as the weather was cold enough to keep it cold. For those who needed a little more to keep them warm there was always a bottle of brandy or whiskey available too. People seemed to rotate from the fires to the water and back the fires again. One must remember in those days we didn't have quality waders or warm clothing we have today. It didn't take long to get cold, wading in Lake Michigan. It was noisy with the waves splashing up on shore, the crackling of drift wood fires, people yelling, laughing and bantering. It was a great party.

There were several different ways to net smelt. There were seines, usually pulled by two or more people on either end of the long nets. There were dip nets, looking much like landing nets but with finer mesh netting. Then there were drop nets. Those were most often used off bridges over the rivers and streams running into Lake Michigan. It was a square net with lead weights to get it down in the current without tipping the net in the water. The net was dropped down with ropes and once hitting the bottom would be rapidly brought up.

Regardless if you were using a seine, dip net or drop net, when you brought the net in it was teaming with flashes of silver from smelt. Most smelt measured about four to six inches. The fish were dumped in buckets and many times one swipe of a net could bring enough smelt to fill a five-gallon bucket. It was phenomenal the amount of smelt netted. In one evening, you could fill enough buckets of smelt to feed an entire church or small town. Which actually happened on a fairly regular basis. They really were that abundant.

One of my buddies told me when he was a kid his father would take him and his brothers to the beaches on Lake Superior to get smelt. They didn't have a net. When the waves washed up on shore it deposited bunches of smelt on the sand so he and his brothers ran out, picking up as many smelt as they could, skipping back up the beach with their smelt in hand before the next wave rolled up on shore, again stranding more smelt. They continued to do this until they had all the smelt they wanted.

Another buddy of mine, living at the time in Milwaukee, would just take a twelve pack of beer and a bucket and drive north until he found a bunch of people standing around on the beach. He traded his beer for a bucket of smelt. Considering his financial status in those days it probably was fairly cheap beer but apparently smelt fishermen weren't particularly discriminating when it came to beer. They were catching more than their share of smelt so it was more than a fair trade. Netting smelt sure could make a man thirsty.

A night of netting smelt could result in bunches of smelt sloshing around in five-gallon buckets and wash tubs. It wasn't uncommon to come home with a trunk or a pickup loaded with smelt. I wonder how long it would take to get the fish smell out of the trunk. Then the next big chore was to clean them. Cleaning them was actually fairly easy. You just needed a scissors. To clean them, cut off the head with the scissors, cut down the belly, scoop out the guts and that was it. Although it was easy, it was long tedious job when you had buckets of smelt to deal with. For many people it became a family or neighborhood project. Aunts, uncles, brothers and sisters, family friends and neighbors sitting around the basement or garage cleaning buckets or washtubs of smelt. Sometimes it took as long to clean them as it was to get them. As a reward people left with buckets of cleaned smelt to have their own smelt fries.

Smelt were so plentiful, men from churches, bars, VFW Halls or American Posts would get a bunch of smelt so their organization or bar could sponsor a smelt fry. Even if you didn't go netting for smelt going to a local smelt fry was part of spring. Of course, bags of smelt were passed out to family and friends and I remember my father one day coming home with a bag of smelt. As the oldest child I was allowed to sit up on Friday nights to watch the horror movies which came on television after the late evening news on one of the three channels we got out of Green Bay. My two younger sisters were a bit miffed they weren't allowed to join us, having been sent off to bed before the news started. As we watched the movies my father always made some snack. That was when I first had pizza. It was a Jess and Nicks frozen pizza. The Friday after Father got the smelt he made them while we watched the horror movies. He rolled them in flour and fried them in butter. I remember them being very tasty.

Unfortunately, the hay day of the smelt run and smelt fries began to die out in the 1970s and 80s. Smelt were no longer in the vast numbers they one had been. By the mid 1960s the lamprey was finally controlled enough so stocking of trout and salmon was possible. There might have been other reasons for the decline of smelt but reintroducing trout and salmon back into the Great Lakes was a major factor. The great schools of alewives, another invasive species to the Great Lakes, were also a principal forage base for trout and salmon and responsible for the tremendous growth rate of those fish. But smelt now had competition from the alewives for food and spawning areas. As smelt were competing with the alewives and once again became bait fish for trout and salmon their numbers dramatically declined. The days of the great smelt runs were now over and with it the huge smelt fries. Today, most of smelt are taken through deep water netting in the Great Lakes.

The Baldwin Fire and Rescue Station has been holding their smelt fry for thirty-eight years. Originally, the Baldwin smelt fry was a community project but the town gave up on the smelt fry a couple of years before the Baldwin Volunteer Fire station took it over. It is their major fund raiser according to Gary Newton, Baldwin Station Chief. It is held in the Baldwin American Legion Post a few blocks from the Fire Station. The Fire Station has thirty-eight volunteer fire fighters covering four villages and ten townships.

When the Fire Station first revived the smelt fry some of the volunteer firemen still went over to Lake Michigan to net smelt but soon after they began to purchase their smelt from a distributor. They initially purchased whole smelt and cleaned them themselves. That became a real chore according to Gary. "If you wanted six hundred pounds of smelt to cook, you had to order twelve hundred pounds of smelt to clean." Gary said. It became a tedious, week-long process. All the fire fighters came into clean fish as well as people from the community. By the end of the week people were getting a bit testy, Gary pointed out. Now they purchase their smelt already cleaned. Their distributor is in Two Rivers and last year they ordered eight hundred and fifty pounds of smelt. "All we had left at the end of the day was one roaster of smelt," Gary said.

The Baldwin smelt fry provides all the smelt you can eat plus chips, coleslaw, beans, pickles and tartar sauce, all for a free will donation. "All of the money goes to purchase equipment," Gary said. Lately they have been purchasing air packs.

"For a couple weeks out, we will be getting phone calls at the station asking about the smelt fry," Gary said. They will receive the smelt earlier in the week and then on Thursday, the day before, they start getting everything organized. Active volunteer fire fighters with many of the retired fire fighters do all the work. For some it is a tradition which can't be missed, requiring the day off their regular jobs to work the smelt fry.

Bob Lokken, from Baldwin, a retired fire fighter handles mixing the breading for the smelt. He told me it is a mixture of water, flour, eggs molasses and baking powder. The tartar sauce is a family recipe from Gary Newton's mother and they will go through over thirty gallons of tartar sauce. They also make their own coleslaw, last year using two hundred and fifty pounds of fresh cut coleslaw.

Friday morning starts out with a breakfast for the

fire fighters at the American Legion Post. It is part of the tradition, Gary explained. Doug Anderson of Baldwin, another retired fire fighter, is the fish cooker and has been doing it for years. At 11:00 they start serving smelt. "People from all over come to the smelt fry," Gary said. People from Menominee twenty miles east to Minnesota's Twin Cities thirty miles west show up for the smelt fry.

Last year when I arrived with two friends from Hudson, the parking lot was filled with cars and a line out the door with people waiting to get in. "We have had people call in twenty or more takeout orders at one time," Gary said. "Some of the factories in the area have whole shifts come over at lunch or dinner time. We've seen people come by for lunch and then return later in the evening for dinner." Last year by 8:00 in the evening when they finished, they had served over eleven hundred people.

The smelt run and smelt fries were all about people having fun. It started that way in the 1950s and 60s and in Baldwin it still is that way thanks to the Baldwin Volunteer Fire and Rescue Station. Gary summed it all up by pointing out "it makes for a fun community day."

THE WORLD-FAMOUS OUTDOOR CATALOG

Before there was Cabela's and Bass Pro Shop catalogs there was the "World Famous" Herter's catalog. Growing up in the late 1950s and 60s it was the final word on any kind of outdoor equipment. They sold everything you could think of; from decoys to boats to outdoor clothing to all the hunting and fishing gear you would ever need. They even sold guns. Yes, you could buy a gun from their catalog and it would be shipped through the mail. If Herter didn't have it, you didn't need it.

The cover of the catalog stated they were "The authentic world source for hunters, fishermen, guides, gunsmiths, law enforcement officers, tackle makers, forest rangers, commercial fishermen, trappers and explores." Although not mentioned but also for teenage boys and other dreamers.

The catalog came out sometime in February as I recall. When it arrived in the mail it broke up winter. I was still shoveling snow out of the driveway. In those days you didn't need a snow blower as long as you had a teenage boy in the family. On top of winter, school was getting real boring by February but the Herter's catalog changed all that. You could come home from school and settle into your bedroom with the Herter's catalog, leaving winter and school behind by paging through the catalog and dream about summer, camping and fishing.

Herter's dates back to 1893 but it didn't become the "Authentic World Source" or "World Famous" until George L. Herter inherited the dry goods store, located in Waseca, Minnesota in 1935 from his father. He started by selling fly tying materials through the mail and just expanded from there. By the 1950s the catalogs were legendary and Herter's was selling just about anything you could possibly need or want for the outdoors.

George Herter wrote all the copy for everything in the catalog. Nothing was too outlandish for him. Everything was "World Famous." Reading the product descriptions was always great fun. If George Herter said it was "World Famous" then by God it had to be true. Thousands of outdoorsmen throughout the country agreed, as did I.

Because we believed in Herter's we bought stuff from him. A lot of stuff. In my bedroom I poured over that catalog. Of course, I wanted it all. But the financial reality of my sole income from cutting lawns during the summer did restrict some of my purchasing power. When I first got the catalog, I would mark the things I wanted. My want list was much bigger than my finances but there was nothing wrong with dreaming. As we got closer to spring, I started to be more realistic in my expectations and bought only those things I truly felt I could afford and would use the most.

In the 1950s and 60s Herter's was the biggest single supplier of outdoor gear in the country. I know I bought my share of stuff from Herter's. My father did too. I started with buying flies from them. They had a color page in the catalog displaying their flies. I didn't know much about fly fishing so I just picked flies with names that sounded good; like Parmachenee Belle, Dusty Miller, Royal Coachman and others. I never caught any trout with them but I still have them and now use them on panfish.

Father and I both got our waders from Herter's and we also got our fishing vests from Herter's. My father wore his out but I still have mine. I used it for years, well into my adult years and now it hangs in my basement. We bought our rain gear from Herter's and creels and just about everything in our cache of outdoor gear Father and I stored in the basement. As I was growing up my basic hunting and fishing attire was blue jeans and the Herter's Guide Association Chamois Cloth Shirt in forest green color.

When my mother wanted to get something for Father for his birthday or Father's Day, she had me select some things from the Herter's catalog. One year she bought him a fly rod from Herter's. I now have Father's fly rod. A few years ago, I returned to one of our favorite brook trout streams in northeastern Wisconsin and used that fly rod.

Later I got into duck hunting and that was when I discovered the utilitarian beauty of Herter's decoys. They truly were "World Famous." Every duck hunter I knew either had Herter's decoys or wanted them. One of my uncles was a duck hunter and he told me once, his dream was to own a complete set of Herter's decoys. I bought a dozen mallard decoys and a dozen bluebill decoys. I used them for years. Eventually the bluebill decoys took quite a beating and I gave them to a brother-in-law. I still have the mallard decoys and although I haven't duck hunted in years and might not duck hunt again, I will never part with them. They are stored under the stairs leading to the basement and I find it comforting to know they are there. I grew up with them and it is nice to know a piece of my boyhood remains.

Herter's was a big part of my young life and growing up I thought Herter's would always be there. As big as it once was in its day, Herter's didn't survive the 1970s. By the late 1960s restrictions in selling guns through the mail made an impact. Also, during the 1960's and 70s George Herter began expanding with several smaller stores around the Mid West. It wasn't the best of financial times and by 1980 Herter's was bankrupt and closed. I had just returned from a tour in Europe with the U. S. Army and called Herter's to make an order. The telephone number I had from one of their last catalogs didn't work. I called the telephone company operator in Waseca and she told me Herter's was out of business. I was shocked. How could this happen to Herter's. It was too big to fail or so I thought. But I had the memories and still some of their "World Famous" gear.

In the 1990s there was an attempt to bring back Herter's. One year at the Minneapolis Sportsman Show I ran into a booth calling themselves Herter's. A couple of young guys bought the Herter's name, specializing in duck hunting gear. They had plans to reissue the decoys. They were at the sportsman show for a couple of years and even published a small catalog. It didn't have George Herter's flair of description but one of items they were selling was a reprint of the 1966 catalog. I had long wished I kept some of those old catalogs so I made about ten hints a day to my wife I wanted the reprinted catalog for Christmas. My wife Becky got the hint, how could she miss it, and when I opened that gift, my boyhood came racing back to me. I sat at the dining room table paging through the catalog and telling her "I got one these" or "I remember this." Unfortunately, after a couple of years the new Herter's disappeared. I was truly disappointed as I really wanted them to make a go of it.

Today, a little of Herter's still remains. Cabela's sells a line of shotgun and handgun ammunition under the Herter's name. On the box of ammo, they use the Herter's logo. The first time I saw the ammo it brought a smile to my face and once again the memories of my life with Herter's.

A couple of years ago I was in an antique/junk shop and as usual I gravitated to the old fishing gear. In one of the displays was a Herter's fiberglass spincasting rod. I had to have it. It cost me twenty-five dollars. In the 1976 catalog (the only one I had kept) it sold for $5.29 and described as "quality, appearance and the right action makes this series of rods the best value on today's market." At another shop I found a Pflueger Supreme casting reel. In the same catalog it also was available for the price of $33.97.

That got me to thinking. I still had a couple baits I bought from Herter's when I was a kid. I thought I needed to fish them. One of the baits was a jigging spoon called Herter's Famous Hudson Bay Jig Lure. George Herter wrote in the catalog this bait "takes walleye, crappies, bass, northern pike fished summer or winter. Out fishes by a wide margin any jig type of lure." How could any fourteen-year-old kid resist buying this bait? I didn't.

A month after getting the old Herter's rod I was on the Mississippi River fishing for walleyes and sauger. I pulled out the Herter's rod and the Pflueger reel now loaded with twelve-pound monofilament line and the Herter's

Famous Hudson Bay Jig Lure attached to it, baited it with a minnow. I let the lured drop to the bottom, lifting it up about a foot and then back to the bottom. I was jigging for about five minutes when a fish slammed it. The fish raced off, bending the Herter's rod in half. The fish put up a stiff fight but a moment or two later I had it splashing next to the boat. It was a keeper size sauger. I planned to use the rod and reel and bait to just catch a fish and then retire it back to the rod locker. But it had been so much fun I spent the rest of the afternoon fishing it and caught several more keeper saugers.

George Herter shamelessly copied other baits, changing the name and calling them his own. A bait looking like the Johnson Silver Minnow he called Herter's Olson Minnow, Al's Goldfish became Herter's French Shiner, a Jitter Bug became the Rock and Roller, a Lazy Ike was Herter's Lazy Dabner to just name a few. Even at fourteen I figured that out so when I bought lures from Herter's I selected something which was different, I hadn't seen before. Of course, his grand claims of how good these baits worked persuaded me as well. The Hudson Bay Jig Lure looked much like a Swedish Pimple but it had little spinners attached to it to make it different. As I found out on the Mississippi it caught fish. George Herter was right.

Another bait which struck my fancy as a young fisherman was the Herter's Winglure. In the catalog George told how it was a special bait being used exclusively for centuries in England and now Herter's could duplicate it. He made it sound as if it was the Holy Grail of baits. How could anyone say no to the Winglure? It was a small spoon with wings at the back of it. The one I have is blue and silver but according to the catalog it was also offered in gold for the incredible price of thirty-seven cents.

One cool, early summer day I decided I needed to catch a fish with the Winglure. I was fishing a lake in northwestern Wisconsin, pulling my boat into a small bay. I knew there were bass and panfish in this bay since I caught them there before. Within half a dozen casts I saw a silver flash in the water and felt a jolt on the line. Setting the hook, the fish took off, swirling on the surface and diving for the weeds. I turned the fish and a moment later had it next to the boat. The fish was a foot long largemouth bass. I felt very satisfied catching a fish on Herter's Winglure, probably half a century after I originally bought it from the Herter's catalog. I continued to fish it as I moved slowly through the bay, catching another three more bass before putting my Winglure away. I sure didn't want some northern pike to come along and tear it off. I am thinking I need to go on the internet to see if I can find the gold version of it and try that too. But I expect I will be paying a lot more than thirty-nine cents for it now.

I always dreamed of visiting the Herter's store in Waseca but never got there and since it closed, I didn't know if there would be anything left of it today. A couple summers ago, my wife and I were in Mankato, Minnesota for a Willie Nelson concert. I've wanted to see Willie for years and finally got the chance. It was warm, summer evening and we drank a couple cold beers while listening to Willie. The next morning, we left to drive back home and once on the road I saw a sign saying Waseca was twenty some miles away. I told Becky about Herter's and my wanting to visit the store there and said something like if we get back this way again, we might arrange to stop in Waseca to see if there are any reminders of Herter's still there. She told me we have all day and there isn't any need to rush back home so why not go there now. With that, I drove past the road I needed to turn on to head home and kept going to Waseca.

Waseca is a small town jutting up out of the Minnesota farm land around it. As we entered the town, I was starting to get excited. I didn't know where to start so I thought the best place to get some information would be the local newspaper office. When we got there, we found the office was closed for lunch. A block up the street I saw a hardware store which might have some information. I walked in, stopping at the checkout. A middle age lady was behind the cash register. I told her a shortened version of my childhood attraction to Herter's and wondered if the Herter's building was still standing and if so, how do I get there. She listened patiently to me and then told me she was fairly new to Waseca and didn't know anything about Herter's but the guy in the in the back of the store with all the nuts and bolts probably did.

When I got to the back of the store, I found an older man she suggested I talk to but he was helping someone. I waited patiently next to the counter waiting for him to get free. A minute or two later an elderly gentlemen came back to the counter. He was looking for a replacement part for a pump. He looked like he was old enough to remember Herter's so I told him my story and asking if there anything left of Herter's. He looked me and said "World Famous." He told me he once worked for Herter's as a young man and said the Herter's building was still standing. With directions from him I went back to the car. I was getting closer.

It still took me a few minutes to find it and eventually drove up to a building with the words Winegar, Inc., on the side of the building. Could this have once been Herter's? I got out of the car and next to a door which led into an office I saw a metal plaque reading "Herter's Since 1893." I was overjoyed. I found it. I went in to the office, approaching two secretaries. I told them my story again and they listened patiently. When I finished one of them told me I needed to see their manager. A few minutes later a man looking like he was in his 50s approached me. I told him my story and when I finished, he smiled and said "World Famous." "It sure was," I said.

He told me he also worked for Herter's when he was a kid. He mentioned that just about everyone in Waseca had something to do with Herter's when he was growing up. He said he even met George Herter once. "He was a short, little man, dressed in work clothes," he said. "I thought he was some guy coming by to get the scrapes." Today Winegar, Inc. is a company specializing in machining. The manager let me look into the main part of the building which in its day was the store room and shipping department for Herter's.

George Herter was something of a recluse. The business seemed to run itself, more or less, and apparently, he had good managers so he didn't need to be present at the store often. He didn't care to draw attention to himself and seldom agreed to let anyone interview or photograph him. He also was a World War Two veteran, awarded a Purple Heart and from what I have read, greatly affected by the war. Today he probably would have been diagnosed with Post Traumatic Stress Disorder. He spent most of his time hunting, fishing and traveling, sending back to the store his mounted trophies. In addition to writing the catalog he also wrote fifteen books which he published and sold through the catalogs. I have a couple of those books. They are a mixture of wild stories, bold claims and unique philosophies with some outdoor and survival tips thrown in. Those books are a great, fun read, still today as it was when I was a kid, regardless if anything in it was factual or not.

Although it has been over forty years since Herter closed its doors, I felt like I finally found it. I just wished Herter's was still in business. George Herter lived quietly and withdrawn, reaching the age of eighty-three and died in Minneapolis in 1994. I wished I had met him. The stories he could have told. He and his Herter's catalog were truly "World Famous."

AFTER WINTER

Snow covers my front lawn but as I look outside, I see a pink flamingo poking up out of the snow. It is time to go fishing.

Before anyone thinks I have been ingesting weird chemicals or have gone completely wacky with the long winter and piles of snow around my house, let me explain. Some years back I became enthralled with those plastic pink flamingos one finds all over Florida. I thought my lawn could use one. I found one, setting it out on the front lawn. From time to time, I move it around the lawn just to amuse my neighbors who probably think I am wacky anyway.

When winter starts my pink flamingo is eventually covered by snow drifts. Once I start to see the flamingo emerge from the snow, as it begins to melt, I feel spring is on its way. Now I am seeing the back of my pink flamingo showing itself as snow starts to disappear.

For me the sight of my flamingo is a sure sign of spring and with it the beginning of open water fishing. It is a direct cause and effect relationship. Seeing the flamingo means I can get out on the Mississippi River.

About the time I saw the flamingo I get a call from my

marine dealer, Warner's Dock in New Richmond, Wisconsin. I call them The Boat Doctor because in addition to selling me my last three boats they also do all the maintenance on my boat, motor and trailer. Two weeks earlier I took my boat in for what I call its spring checkup and they just called to tell me my boat is ready to go fishing.

I already have a fishing trip planned. Walleyes and sauger should be hitting on the Mississippi River. It is time to go fishing.

Once in the garage, I charge both the starting and trolling motor batteries although they didn't need much charging since they survived the winter fairly well. I put the big thirty-pound anchor in the boat. I seldom use an anchor any other time of the year except when fishing the Mississippi River. It is the biggest anchor I can find and sometimes it isn't even enough for the strong currents in the Mississippi River, swollen with the runoff from melting snow.

Next, I load heavy clothes in my vehicle. When fishing the Mississippi River in early spring I dress as if I am going ice fishing. My fishing buddy, Dennis tells me the coldest he has ever been in his adult life was with me in the spring on the Mississippi. Sitting in an aluminum boat on frigid water as a cold wind, sometimes laced with snow and ice, blowing out of the north is as harsh as any day on the ice.

In the back of my vehicle I put insulated bibs, a Gortex jacket to wear over a down jacket, fleece pullover sweater, hooded sweatshirt, and a wax cloth Stormy Kromer hat, a pair of neoprene boots and several pairs of gloves. There are days in the spring when even all this isn't enough.

Then comes the fishing equipment. I bring up the tackle

box with the heavy jigs and sinkers I use in the spring. I seldom ever use anything lighter than an ounce since the trick is to get your bait to the bottom and keep it there despite runoff, swollen water and strong currents.

I have one spinning combo rigged with a three-way rig similar to the Wolf River Rig, except I replace the bell-shaped sinker with an ounce chartreuse jig. Another spinning rod has a three-quarter ounce fire tiger colored blade spoon and another with a chartreuse Fireball Jig by Northland. You can see a pattern here. All the baits have chartreuse. It is the one color which seems to always work in the murky water found in the Mississippi River.

I also have a couple casting rod combos with a three-foot-long leader with a hook and some chartreuse beads below a heavy bell-shaped sinker. The sinker can be as heavy as three ounces to get the bait to bottom in the worst spring current.

These are packed in the rod lockers with spare rods placed in rod racks in the garage. Then of course I check the rest of the boat, insuring I have three life vests, extra gloves and a stocking cap. In a box under the counsel, I have my camera, sun glasses and all the other odds and ends I use from day to day.

The boat is ready. So am I. It is time to go fishing.

I start to watch the weather. On the day we are going fishing the forecast calls for mild temperatures with possible rain and perhaps a bit of snow. What else would I expect? It is spring and the first fishing trip of the year on open water.

My fishing buddy Dennis shows up to tell me it snowed all the way from his house in Burnsville, Minnesota to just before he crossed into Wisconsin. We attach the trailer and boat, load Dennis' clothes and our lunch in my vehicle and head south for the Mississippi River. Just as we get close to the landing a light snow begins drifting down. Skies are gray but it looks like little or no wind. It is a good feeling to see the boat slide off the trailer into the water. I have waited all winter for this day.

There doesn't seem to be a lot of boats out today. At the landing there are only eleven vehicles with boat trailers. We heard the fishing has been slow but it the first time on open water so we don't care about the reports. It is just good to be fishing.

We head upriver, towards the dam a few miles north of Red Wing, Minnesota. We find only three other boats just below the dam. As we are slowly moving toward the bank, we see one boat with three fishermen in it. One guy is fighting a fish and as we pass them one of the other fishermen leans over, grabs into the water, pulling a large brown catfish into the boat. This is a good omen.

There is a rocky island splitting the lock and dam with the lock on the Minnesota side of the river and the dam on the Wisconsin side. I slowly motor the boat close to the island on the dam side. The rollers are down on the dam and it looks like the current is not as strong as we normally see this time of year. We are in a little over twenty feet of water when I tell Dennis to drop the anchor. The boat swings around with the current and the anchor rope tightens as the anchor digs in. Snow spits from the sky.

We bait hooks and drop our baits into the water. I am using a three-way rig with an ounce jig and Dennis is using a three-quarter ounce Fireball jig with a stinger hook. Both baits easily get to the bottom and stay there.

Fifteen minutes later the boat which caught the catfish drifts by. We ask how big the catfish was and they tell us it measured thirty-five inches. We congratulate them and ask if they caught anything else. They tell us the fishing is slow and have only two fish in their livewell. One was caught in over forty feet of water and the other in over thirty feet.

The rule of thumb when fishing the river is when the water is high. fish shallow and if normal or low, fish deep. I define twenty feet of water as the dividing line between deep or shallow water. The river is now just a bit above normal so I feel we will be alright where we are and besides, over the years I have caught a lot of fish at this spot close to the bank. But talking to those guys does make me wonder if perhaps fish are in much deeper water right now.

As I am working this over in my mind, I feel a light tap and when I bring up my line, I see I lost a minnow. I might have had a light strike I tell Dennis. Ten minutes later I feel a lot stronger strike and pulling back to set the hook I feel a fish pulling away. I quickly turn the fish and a moment later lead it into the net. The fish is a walleye and it looks big enough to keep. I measure the fish and it is just over fifteen inches. On the Mississippi River walleyes have a minimum size limit of fifteen inches while sauger do not have any size restrictions. The walleye goes into the livewell. Dennis wants to take a meal of fish home with him.

Although we are fishing for walleyes and sauger you can catch just about anything in the Mississippi River. In the spring we see a lot of catfish and sturgeon. It is not uncommon to catch crappies, yellow perch, northern pike, even a muskie from time to time and over the years we have even caught a couple of brown trout. Later in April when the white bass move in it is not unusual to catch a hundred fish per boat per day.

A couple more boats show up at the dam but we don't see any fish being caught. We stop for lunch and decide after lunch we will give this spot another half hour and if we get nothing, we will move across the channel to the Wisconsin bank. We resume fishing and the next thing we notice is the boat is moving. I check to find the anchor broke loose. We find ourselves in a little over thirty feet of water when we drop the anchor again. We did say we wanted to move. We fish there for about a half hour without a strike.

Dennis pulls the anchor in as I maneuver the boat back to where we had been but this time move a little further out into a bit deeper water. We drop anchor in about twenty-seven feet of water and the current swings us back and forth from twenty-five to twenty-eight feet. The current is still not very strong.

We hear the deep guttural honking of geese and look up to see a string of Canada geese working northward against the wind. Above them is a flock of snow geese yelping. Around us we see eagles twisting and turning in the sky above us, others sitting in trees screeching at each other. I look upriver towards the dam to see an eagle set its wings, glide just above the water and pluck out a fish before it swings up, away from the water. Everything comes alive on the Mississippi River during the spring.

We notice the snow has stopped. The winds remain light. It is pleasant sitting in the boat today but Dennis and I dressed for the worst weather and are comfortable. We talk of other days on the river in the spring, recalling sitting on the water in blizzards and ice storms with line freezing in the rod guides. Today is a pleasant exception.

I feel another hard tap on my line as a fish races off. This is a bigger fish and I yell for Dennis to grab the net. It puts up a tougher battle by the time Dennis pulls the net up with the fish sagging in the mesh. It is an eighteen-inch sauger, swollen with spawn already starting to leak out. I twist the hook out, slipping the fish back in the water. I feel guilty about putting the fish back but hate to kill a spawning fish in the spring although I know Dennis wants a fish fry.

We notice the wind picks up a bit but is still fairly mild and the current seems to be getting stronger.

Half an hour later another fish hits. This fish is another walleye, a bit bigger than the first one we kept so it goes into the livewell. Dennis now has enough fish for a Friday night fish fry so I feel better; no more guilt about releasing the sauger knowing we have the fish fry covered.

We discuss changing spots again but notice no one is catching any more fish than we are. We decide to stay put since we are catching some fish.

A fish surges off with my bait. This is no tentative strike. It slammed it. "Big fish," I yell to Dennis. My spinning rod is bent in half and the tip is plunging. The fish runs off and I stop it, starting to get it coming toward the boat but it keeps darting off. Slowly I get the fish closer and we can now see it. Dennis gets the net under the fish, pulling it in the boat. It is a big walleye, thick and feisty. It measures twenty-one inches. I get the hook out, taking a photo before I slip it back in the water.

As Dennis and I return to the landing we are happy. It is our first day on open water after what has been a long winter. The weather was fairly nice for this time of the year, we weren't skunked and Dennis got a fish fry. Can't ask for much more from the first fishing trip.

A BOAT WITH A LIFETIME OF MEMORIES

You don't see them much anymore but there was a day when boats were made of wood. Boats by Chris Craft, Dunphy, and Century were and still are legendary throughout the Mid West and were pieces of floating artwork.

The names and boats have disappeared over the years and been lost to history and deterioration. By the end of the 1960s and beginning of the 1970s many of those proud companies had abandoned wood boats for fiberglass and the days of those beautiful old boats were numbered.

Sadly, many of those once powerful and sleek wood boats were parked behind garages and barns or in some field where the elements, over time, would destroy the remains of their legacy.

But every, now and then, one of those old wood boats survived. A rare few have been cared for over the years and stored properly and brought out on the water now and then. Others have been found and restored to live again.

Once such boat, a Century, still races across the water of Deer Lake in Wisconsin's Polk Country. It is a story of survival, a family and a love for a boat, once lost but now resurrected.

In 1965, Emil Jandric bought and launched a brand new eighteen-foot Century Sabre on Turtle Lake in Shoreview, Minn. It was a thing of beauty and power described by Century Boat Company as a small, sporty runabout. The family's nine children fell in love with the boat and they raced and skied across the lake with that boat all summer long.

"I skied behind that boat for five or six hours a day," Frank "Bucky" Jandric recalled from the days of his youth. That 1965 wood Century became an important part of his and his family's summer as he was growing up.

However, everything in life changes and in 1971 Emil sold the boat to a man across the lake. "The family was devastated," Bucky recalls but as he put it "life goes on" as the kids in the family were getting older and leaving home. Five years later the man who bought the boat from Bucky's father sold it to another person who lived on the lake. He was a pilot and when he was reassigned to Seattle, Wash., he took the boat with him. It looked like the boat was gone for good.

Century Boat Company began in 1926 by two brothers in Milwaukee, Wisconsin, who developed wooden hulls designed for speed. Two years later Century Boat Company moved to Manistee, Mich., where it remained for the next 60 years. In 1930 a boat built by Century set a world speed boat record by going 50.93 miles per hour.

During the Second World War, Century built 3,600 boats for the military. By 1950 they were back in the pleasure boat business with over 343 dealers across the country using the slogan "The Thoroughbred of Boats." More changes were coming in the 1960s and in 1967 the last wooden boat was built by Century Boats as they transitioned to making fiberglass boats.

Bucky and his family never forgot their Century boat. Twenty years later they wondered what happened to the boat and started to look for it.

"My brother Bill was the one who found it," Bucky said. Bill contacted the man who bought the boat from their father and later sold it to the pilot. From him he got the name of the pilot and tracked him down in Washington.

He still had the boat but it hadn't been used in years and was stored outside where the elements were eating away at the once elegant boat.

Bucky finally decided he had to do something about it and contacted the pilot, offering to buy the boat. It had been stored outside and not used in at least ten years. He was warned the boat was in bad shape but went ahead with it anyway, shipping the boat by truck back to Minnesota. When Bucky saw the boat, he realized it came as advertised and was in bad shape but determined to have it restored.

He found Harold Thompson, in Nisswa, Minnesota, who had worked for Century since he was 20 and now in his old age restored boats because of his love for the old wooden boats. But even he was a bit pessimistic.

He put his hands on Bucky's shoulders and said "Son, you sure you want to do this. It will never be worth what you will have in it." Bucky recalled.

"It wasn't about the money I told him." Bucky said. "It was about the memories and about legacy."

For the next year and a half Harold tore the boat apart,

replacing parts and lovingly put the boat back together. The best part of the restoration process was "working with Harold," Bucky stated. He loved what he was doing Bucky explained. "I became his runner," he said. He was finding and ordering parts Harold needed and delivered them to him. "It was fun to bring something back to life."

"I just wanted it done in my dad's lifetime," Bucky said.

Even the motor, a 240 horsepower Ford Interceptor was rebuilt to like when it was new.

As it turned out it would be one of the last boats Harold would work on. By the summer of 1998 the work was completed and the boat completely resorted. Bucky brought the boat to his house on Deer Lake in northwestern Wisconsin and unveiled it on August 5, 1998, during a family gathering on his father's birthday.

When his father saw the boat, he was a "little teary eyed" Bucky recalled. The whole family went out on the boat again and it brought back those long-ago days of their childhood. "It was just like we were kids again," Bucky said. "As soon as they got out of sight everyone just stomped on it" as they raced once across the water.

In the 1980s Century Boat Company was sold to a couple different companies and underwent a number of changes to include building another production facility in Panama City. In 1995 Century was purchased by Yamaha and in 2009, their last year with Yamaha, when they finally ceased production, they still had forty-five dealers in eighteen states. In 2012 Allcraft Marine in Dade City, Florida, purchased Century with plans to introduce a newline of Century boats in 2013.

Bucky's 1965 Century boat survives as well with his

family preserving a bit of the once sleek and elegant line of wood Century boats. Bucky told me every time he drives his boat across Deer Lake he is "reliving my childhood." His boat is a thing of beauty and when it races across the water most fishermen stop to watch it go past. The motor has a deep, powerful rumble to it which is a pleasant change from the whine of today's outboards.

Emil, the original owner, passed away three years ago but his son, Bucky and the rest of his family maintain the legacy and tradition their Century Sabre represents and will someday pass it on to another generation of their family.

THE JOYS OF APRIL

It is easy for fishermen to overlook the month of April. The regular fishing season doesn't start until the first Saturday in May so no one gets too excited about April. It is just another month to get through until fishing season starts. Although some fishermen may ignore April there is a lot going on that month which makes for great fishing.

My first memories of fishing in April were the famed walleye run on the Wolf and Fox Rivers. I remember Friday nights after supper, my father and I would drive to Winneconne where my father knew a man who had a small engine repair shop right on the river which also included a dock on the water. Getting to the dock after dark, we set out our lines and waited for a walleye to come through.

I remember the nights being cold. We could hear the river rushing by in the darkness. On the river there would be some boats bobbing around on the water with lights reflecting off the surface and fishermen would be lined up on the bridge which crossed the river. Lanterns would be lit and lines dangled down from the bridge. It seemed like the fishermen on the bridge were just one big party. Maybe it was just a party to some of them.

Everyone seemed to know each other and there was a great deal of comrade among all the fishermen or perhaps it just a shared experience of enduring the cold and wind when the fish weren't hitting. Regardless if the fish were hitting or not there always seemed to be a lot of excitement. I guess a lot of people were happy to just get out fishing.

Father would send me over to a bar, grill and bait shop next to the dock to get hot coffee for him and hot chocolate for me. We got a bucket of minnows there earlier when we first started fishing. Going back to get hot drinks I remember the smell of grease and hamburgers from the grill mixing with beer and stale cigarette smoke from the bar mingling with the odors from the minnow tanks.

I never remembered catching a lot of fish. Like everyone else we were just happy to be fishing. One night Father put his rod down on the dock while he was drinking his coffee when his line shot out. He grabbed his spinning rod just before it was going to be dragged into the water. His spinning rod was bent in half as he fought the fish, finally flipping it up on the dock. It was about a thirty-inch northern pike. A few minutes later my rod tip began to bounce and when I set the hook, I felt a fish pulling away. It turned out to be a walleye and half an hour later I added a white bass to the bucket. It was probably our best night of fishing the river in April.

Now I live on the other side of the Wisconsin near the Mississippi River and once again I am fishing for walleyes and sauger in April. When we start in early April there may be people in northern Wisconsin and Minnesota still ice fishing, but the river is open and the fish are running. I am happy to be out on open water in a boat again after a long winter. It still feels a lot like winter and I am dressed as if I am ice fishing. In April on the Mississippi, I have been through ice storms and blizzards but they are a mere inconvenience in comparison to the joys of fishing again on the river.

I fish the dam on the Mississippi River north of Red Wing, Minnesota. I use a modified version of the Wolf River Rig my father and I used when I was a kid. The Wolf River Rig begins with a three-way swivel. One swivel has a leader with a bell-shaped sinker and another swivel has a longer leader with a hook. Now when I fish my version of the Wolf River Rig, I replace the bell-shaped sinker with a one-ounce chartreuse jig and on the hook leader I add three chartreuse beads with a chartreuse hook. I normally bait both the jig and hook with minnows but there are times now when I will use a three- or four-inch plastic grub on the jig.

I remember once on the first of April. My buddy Doug Hurd of Eagan, Minnesota and I were on the Mississippi River. It was our first day on the river. It was chilly with gray skies and the promise of more snow to come. Fish were hitting steadily and we were putting a few fish in the livewell. They were mostly sauger with an occasional walleye. Anytime you are fishing a river and especially the Mississippi River you never know what you will catch when you set the hook.

Early afternoon a fish slammed my bait. When I set the hook, it felt like I was hung up except I could feel throbbing on the other end of the line. The fish began to move and there was nothing I was going to do to stop it. My drag was singing and my line was slicing through the water. I started to chase after the fish with my trolling motor. Sometimes I could pull the fish up a couple of feet but then it would just sink back to the bottom. Every time I got the fish coming up toward the boat it just moved off seeming merely inconvenienced by my hook and line.

It was probably about fifteen minutes before I finally got the fish off the bottom but the fight was far from over. Ten minutes later the fish was just below the surface but with the muddy water we still hadn't seen it yet. I pulled back on the rod, surprised my eight-pound ten line was still holding, and then we saw it. It was a huge catfish and it looked almost frightening as it boiled to the surface. We figured it was a big fish but this one looked almost prehistorically huge.

Doug grabbed the net but we knew it was never going to fit in it. I had some rubber gloves in the boat and with those Doug grabbed the fish on either side of the head by the gills, trying to drag it into the boat but couldn't get it in. Dropping my spinning rod, I wrapped my arms around Doug's waist and we both pulled the fish into the boat. The catfish was about four feet long and between a foot to foot and a half wide. Doug took my photo and I had to use both hands to just barely hold the fish up. I guessed it weighed close to fifty pounds. When I put it back in the water the fish just slowly swam away. My eight-pound line was twisted and kinked. I cutoff about thirty feet before I could use it again.

Doug and I continued to catch saugers with the occasional walleye. Some were too small and they went back in the river but we were catching enough keepers to put in the livewell for a future fish fry. Doug set the hook and his spinning rod was bucking as he brought the fish in.

As he got it to the surface he said "what is this?" Hoisting it in the boat we saw it was a foot long brown trout. You can catch a bit of everything when fishing the river. We ended the day with almost fifty fish. In addition to the big catfish, the wayward brown trout and a bunch of smaller sauger and walleye we released, we kept ten fish. That night it began to snow and the next morning we found a foot of snow on the ground. It would be a couple of days before we got back on the river.

One of the other joys of April is early season perch fishing. Our family gathers at our daughter, Kim Aguilar's house for Easter. She, her husband Damien and their children live in an eastern suburb of Minneapolis. Our other daughter Lisa Hein and her children, living in La Crosse, come up for the holiday. The Saturday before Easter is prep time for Easter dinner but also our annual perch fishing trip. Damien comes out to our hometown of Hudson, bringing along the oldest two grandchildren Max and Amelia Hein. We start the day with going out to get a hamburger and then head to Lake Mallalieu.

Lake Mallalieu separates the town of Hudson from North Hudson. In the middle 1800s a dam was built on a river running into the St Croix and the resulting back up of water became Lake Mallalieu. The lake was used to store logs rafted down the river from the logging camps further north and to provide pressure to run the saw mills at the mouth of the river. Today the saw mills are long gone but the lake is still there and I have been fishing it for over the twenty years I made Hudson my home. The lake is primarily known for bass fishing, both smallmouth as well as largemouth, but the season for those fish is still a month away so instead we go for yellow perch.

We slowly motor over the lake to where the water slides over the dam. In front of the dam is an old railroad bridge. It hasn't been used as long as I have lived in Hudson but once it led to the entrance of one of the largest box car repair facilities in the country. I turn the motor off as we near the bridge and float up to the bridge as I crawl to the front of the boat and Damien is standing on the back casting deck. I grab the rough logs of the bridge and tie off the front of the boat as Damien ties off the back. Fishing is easy. We put small crappie minnows on light jigs, dropping them to the bottom and jigging them slightly.

Damien catches the first perch. The tip of his ultralight spinning rod is bouncing as the fish pulls away but within a moment, he has the fish splashing alongside the boat. Within a couple of minutes Max brings in a perch and before he has baited his hook again, his sister Amelia flips a perch into the boat. From there the fish continue to hit and the action is fast and furious. The perch hit our baits hard. There is no mistaking a strike and put up a tough fight on light spinning rods.

When the fish begin to slow down, we untie the boat, pull ourselves along the bridge and tie back up twenty feet or so from where we started. The fishing starts all over again. At one time Damien, Max and Amelia caught a fish at the same time. It just doesn't get any better than that. We end the day catching about seventy perch. A third of them we could have kept if we were interested in a fish fry but no one wants to clean fish the day before Easter so we release all of our fish.

One year on our annual Day Before Easter Perch Fishing trip we heard Max yell he had a big fish. Of course, there are bass in the lake so as Max was battling his fish with his ultralight spinning rod doubled over, I expected to see him bring in a smallmouth or largemouth which would have been hanging around the piles of the bridge. Max kept cranking on the reel as the fish raced off and Max stopped the fish, turning it toward the boat again. The fish made a couple more runs before Max finally had the fish on the surface.

I saw a flash which looked silvery and I yelled for Damien to grab the net. Damien thrust the net in the water and pulling it up we saw Max had a large trout. It was a brown trout and we estimated it went about four pounds. It was quite a trophy for a thirteen-year-old boy. We took a couple of photos before Max lowered the fish back into the water. The river draining into Lake Mallalieu is known as a trout stream so probably because the water is so cold in the lake in April, with the ice coming off only a week or so earlier, would have lured the big brown out of the river into the lake.

By the mid to late April crappies will start moving into shallow water. It might be the best time of the year to catch a bunch of them. I always plan a couple crappie fishing trips in the last weeks in April. It was a warm April day when my buddy Dennis Virden, of Burnsville, Minnesota and I drove to Loveless Lake in Wisconsin's Polk County. I fished this lake off and on for years and knew there were crappies there. We didn't need a lot of crappies. Another fishing buddy was supposed to join us for the day but he was having health problems so he had to back out. Dennis and

I decided we needed to get enough crappies for our buddy to have a fish fry.

We launched the boat and motored across the lake to where there is a stretch of bank with fallen timber, submerged logs and over hanging brush. You can always find crappies in places like that, especially in April. We didn't bother with minnows. Instead, we were going to use small tube jigs. We pulled up to the first sunken tree and dropped the trolling motor. Casting our jigs toward the tree and just as the jig hit deeper water right off the brush, we felt a pop and setting the hook our ultralight spinning rods came a live as a fish surged off. Some of the fish were smaller than we wanted but they all put up a short, spectacular fight. We caught and released about half a dozen crappies before we moved to the next log or pile of brush. Where ever we paused we picked up at least a couple fish.

Dennis pulled up on his spinning rod and announced he thought he had a bigger fish. I watched and a couple moments later we saw a silvery flash in the water just before Dennis hoisted the fish into the boat. It is a keeper size crappie and went into the livewell. As we work along the bank, we caught a few yellow perch and some bluegills. But we are intent on crappie so those fish went back into the water.

We stop for lunch and the wind gently drifts us across the late as we eat our sandwiches. It is warm and sunny and we are enjoying the weather as much as the fishing. It is hard to believe it still was snowing at the beginning of the month. We move along the brushy bank and continue to catch panfish, slowly putting a few more crappies in the livewell. By midafternoon we caught over sixty fish and have enough fish in the livewell so our ailing friend will have a fish fry sometime in the next few days. It had been another great day in April.

April has much going for it. The regular fishing season might start in May but good fishing has been going on for over a month starting in April. From winter making its last stand in the first of April to the warm days of spring at the end of the month there is lot of fishing going on. The joy of April is to once again get out on open water.

PLASTICS JUNKIE

Plastics dominate bass fishing. It is hard to think of bass fishing without plastic baits. Go to any fishing department you will generally find more rows devoted to plastic baits than all other baits combined. They come in all shapes, sizes and colors. There are plastic lizards, frogs, crawdads, various minnow like baits and of course plastic worms. I'm sure there are other plastic baits I haven't thought of but someone else has. They come in a mind numbing array of colors which doesn't match any living bait I have seen. But they all catch fish, someplace, sometime.

I grew up in east central Wisconsin in the 1950s and 60s where I first fished for bullheads, followed a few years later by walleyes and then eventually trout. I started out with live bait like real worms and nightcrawlers before graduating to artificial baits such as spoons, spinners and what we called plugs. When I needed live bait, I went out to the garden and dug up worms and nightcrawlers. Other than the occasional smallmouth bass we caught by accident we never considered actually bass fishing.

That wasn't the case down south. They always were bass

fishing so it is no surprise fishing with plastic baits would catch on down south first. However, the first successful plastic worm actually came from the Mid West. Nick Crème is considered the father of plastic worms and after the Second World War, he began experimenting with plastic worms in his basement in Akron, Ohio. Sometime in 1949 Nick finally developed a plastic worm he liked and started to produce them for sale in 1951 as the Crème Lure Company. They sold five worms to a pack for one dollar then. They were initially offered through the mail but a Crème lure distributor sold over nine thousand pack of worms at the Cleveland Sport Show and the world of fishing in general and bass fishing in particular has never the same again. In the late 1950's Crème moved to Tyler, Texas, where they are still today.

It didn't take long before other companies sprang up making and selling plastic worms. Another early pioneer in plastic worms was the Mann's Jelly Worm starting in 1967. They are sold in colors like grape, strawberry and other flavors which actually taste like the jelly flavor of which ever worm you choose if you bite into one. From there adding scent to plastic baits took off and now we have garlic, lard, salt and other additives to plastic baits. That is not to mention the other scents which can be added by spaying on plastic baits.

I remember buying my first plastic worm sometime in the early 1960s. It was a three-inch worm in a light brown, worm-like color with a hook in the back and small helicopter spinner on the front. I never had much luck with it but one day I was fishing off a dock at Winneconne and a small yellow perch come out from under the dock and hit it.

I missed the fish but I was in awe that a plastic worm would interest a fish. That was my first exposure to a plastic bait and my last for a number of years.

Then I joined the Army and ended up in Alabama. I started bass fishing with crankbaits. They weren't much different than the baits I used for trolling for walleyes so I was familiar with them. But then, of course, I got involved with plastic worms. At first, I was a bit intimidated with plastic worms because some bass fishermen were carrying on as to how difficult they were to use. Later on, I heard the same stories on jig fishing for walleyes and dry fly fishing for trout. But by then, I learned some fishermen just enjoy making things sound more difficult than they actually are.

It didn't take long before I became addicted to plastic worms. It was crazy. It seemed I had to have a pack of every color they made just in case that one color was going to be the right color when no other color worked. My favorite worm in those days was a seven-inch motor oil color worm with either a chartreuse or orange curly tail. Even with that I had a couple tackle boxes of worms plus several plastic bins of worms with every color imaginable.

Most of my plastic worm fishing was a Texas rig where the hook is pulled through the head of the worm with the tip of the hook buried into the worm an inch or so below the head. Plastic worms float so with the Texas rig we used a bullet shaped sinker to get the plastic worm to the bottom. Also, by this time the pig and jig became big. Of course, I had to try it and one afternoon in the middle of a winter day with snow flurries spitting out of the sky, which is about the most snow they get in Alabama, I caught a four-pound bass on a pig and jig. Most fishermen, in those days for some reason, considered the pig and jig primarily a winter bait. Then the Do-Nothing worm came out. The worm was about the size of a cigarette with two hooks imbedded in it and a small monofilament line with a loop on the end. It was rigged on a four-inch leader attached to swivel with an egg-shaped sinker above the swivel. You simply cast it out and retrieved it slowly. When a fish hit you didn't set the hook but just started reeling it in faster. Naturally, I had to buy a bunch of them. By this time there were lizards, crawdads, frogs and other baits coming out. I could see this was getting out of hand.

After four and a half years in Alabama I was reassigned to the Appalachian Mountains to teach ROTC at a college in North Carolina. They didn't have much bass fishing there, instead there was a lot of trout fishing. It probably was a good thing I was out of bass fishing. Who knows how many more tons of plastic worms I might have bought? Then I went to Germany where I predominately trout fished. After Europe I was back in the states and assigned to Fort Snelling in between Minneapolis and Saint Paul, Minnesota in the last two years before retiring from the Army. Being a Cheesehead I had to come back to Wisconsin and shortly after retiring, my wife and I bought a home in Hudson just across the Wisconsin boarder. There I could get all the Packer games on television.

It was then I discovered western Wisconsin has some of the best bass fishing in the country. Now, all the good old boys I knew from down south were questioning my sanity but they did that anyway when they found out I lived in the country where it snowed for several months every year. "What's wrong with you, boy?" They asked. Try explaining the concept of ice fishing to someone down south. They don't believe people really drill holes through the ice to fish, let alone live there. None of them believe a place that cold could actually have bass. But western Wisconsin does have better bass fishing than anything I found in my years down south.

I was back to bass fishing again. I started out for several years fishing nothing but crankbaits. I had a couple tackle boxes and several more storage boxes devoted to nothing but crankbaits. Then I slowly worked back into spinnerbaits. I am amazed how many spinnerbaits I acquired. I shied away from plastic baits. I knew how addictive they could become. But eventually I got sucked back into plastic baits.

It started innocently enough. I was using a slider head with a short plastic worm. I had slider heads from my days living in Alabama. Instead of using a bullet shaped sinker sliding on my line above a plastic worm like with a Texas rig, the slider head was a flat jig I threaded a plastic worm on. My wife Becky and I were fishing a small creek which entered a lake we were on. It was tough to fish either a crankbait or spinnerbait in such a confined area so I dug around in my boat, found slider heads and plastic worms. That day we caught a dozen and a half bass. I enjoyed seeing a bass hit a plastic bait again. There was sometimes a light bump, other times just weight or a slight jump in the line or the line just moving off. I was getting hooked.

From there I discovered plastic tube jigs for smallmouth bass. We used three-inch plastic tubes with a quarter ounce jig. I started catching lots of smallmouth bass in a couple lakes in northern Wisconsin. It was all I used for smallies. Once I had a problem with a reel. I worked on it, got it fixed and a day or two later was on a largemouth bass lake near my home. That rod had a tube jig on it and I thought I would just take a couple casts to test out the reel. I was fishing a rocky point where I normally used crankbaits but in the next five casts I caught five bass and then on the sixth cast I had a strike but missed the fish. The rest of the day I used the tube jig and caught bass all over that lake. At this point I was using crankbaits about seventy five percent of the time and spinnerbaits about fifteen percent with plastic baits less than ten percent. That was about to change. Suddenly tube jigs were my favorite bait for both largemouth and smallmouth.

For some reason I don't recall I shied away from Texas rigged plastic worms. It was what I used the entire time I lived in Alabama and although I was working myself back into using plastics, I couldn't generate much enthusiasm for the Texas rig. However, on one lake near my home in Hudson I found the Texas rig still worked. This lake had lots of cover all along the shore but after fishing it a couple times with crankbaits I didn't catch many fish. I switched to spinnerbaits and caught a few more but the water looked too good not to have more fish.

Out of desperation one afternoon I was going through my tackle box and ran across the makings of a Texas rig. I had some of the worms I once used in Alabama, long shank worm hooks and a few sliding bullet shaped sinkers. Why not, I thought as I tied a Texas rig to my line. I baited it with a Grape-colored six-inch worm with a red ribbon tail. A dozen casts later I felt weight on my line and pulled back to set the hook. It was my first bass of the day. By late afternoon I caught and released half a dozen bass ranging from a foot to fourteen inches. It still wasn't a lot of fish but more fish than I caught in any one day on that lake before. The Texas rig was riding again.

Then I found sinking worms and my life was about to change. Most plastic baits require a sinker of some sort or a jig to get them to sink. Not with the sinking worms. The plastic is dense enough in sinking worms for them to sink on their own without any additional weight. They gently drop through the water with a side-to-side movement. Bass love these worms. I first started to use the sinking worms, rigged Texas style. I caught lots of fish that way but soon discovered wacky worms.

Wacky worms are sinking worms hooked through the middle of the worm so the two ends of the worm move back and forth as it drops through the water or as it is slowly retrieved with short lifts of the rod tip. I started out by just threading the hook through the middle of the worm but fisherman can't leave anything alone and it didn't take long before someone began placing an O-ring in the middle of the worm, inserting the hook through the O-ring. I heard about this and gave it a try. This was even better and I didn't lose as many worms as I did before with the hook through the middle.

I started catching fish like crazy with wacky worms. This is when things got a bit crazy. Suddenly I found the only bait I was using was the wacky worm. One of my buddies said to me one day, "what, no crankbaits." I wasn't even packing crankbaits in the boat any longer. Now I was catching eighty percent of my fish on wacky worms, and the remaining fish on other baits such as crankbaits or spinnerbaits. It was a complete turnaround.

I also found myself buying lots of worms. It was even

more addictive than it was years ago. I buy all my sinking worms from a guy I call The Worm Dude. I had about half a dozen colors I predominately used with one color in particular called watermelon candy. It was a green worm with speckled flakes in it and I caught most of my fish with it. You would have thought that would be enough but no it wasn't.

I knew of the addictive nature buying plastic worms can be and although I was honesty trying to keep it simple it just wasn't working for me. Every time The Worm Dude got a new color, he would say to me "look at this" and then I would tell him to give me a fifty pack of those. This was getting out of hand again. I had one tackle box stuffed with plastic worms and then another to carry the other colors I was always buying.

I was still catching most of my fish with the watermelon candy but I had enough other colors to open my own bait shop. When my young teen age grandson Max Hein was fishing with me, he would rummage through the other worms and finally pull out a bag of worms, asking me if I thought they would work. We tried them and caught fish with them. It finally dawned on me no matter what color we used we still caught fish. There probably should be some rehab program to help fishermen who become obsessed with buying too many plastic worms. By sheer will power I pulled myself back from the brink of disaster. Now I seldom buy any other colors no matter how good they might look.

About four years ago I stumbled upon the finesse worm craze. Do we really need any more plastic baits? I guess so. The Ned rig caught my attention first. It is essentially a quarter ounce half-moon jig with a three-inch worm. Now there are special Ned rig plastics, but in an effort to develop some discipline, I found these Ned rig baits were about the size of half a normal sinking worm so I started cutting them in half for Ned rigs. Each sinking worm gave me two Ned rig baits.

Then there was the Doug rig. My buddy Doug Hurd kicked my butt with a small sixteenth once jig with a thin four-inch plastic worm. He said he saw it on television or read about it. I'm sure there might be a real name for it but I called it the Doug rig after my buddy who introduced it to me. Again, I was trying to maintain some sense of self-control so I only use four colors of worms. I am very proud of myself for that.

One of the things I have discovered is that no matter what plastic bait or rig you are using, fishing them is truly simple. Just let the bait drop to the bottom and bring it back by lifting the rod tip a foot or so. It works all the time so I guess there is some simplicity after all to using plastic baits.

Last year I discovered the drop shot. It has been a game changer for me. I noticed by midsummer the wacky worms and finesse rigs I had been using weren't catching as many fish. The fish were certainly not in the shallow water I was fishing. How could this be? I have spent a minor fortune on plastic baits and they weren't working. If the fish weren't in the shallow water they must be in deeper water. Most plastic worms can be tough to fish in deep water so I had to find something that could go deep and that was the drop shot.

Rigging the drop shot is simple. There are special drop shot hooks and sinkers but again I'm trying to keep it simple. At the end of your line tie on a swivel slipping on either an eighth or quarter ounce bell shaped sinker. The swivel makes it easier to change sinkers. Eight inches to a foot above the sinker tie on a long shank worm hook with a Palomar knot. That's it. I positioned my boat in fifteen to twenty feel of water and cast toward the outside edge of the weeds. The fishing I found, even in the heat of the summer, was nothing short of phenomenal. I was catching fish in water I had never fished before. Those fish I was catching were bigger and coming from deeper, cold water they put up a great fight.

For drop shot fishing I was finally using up all those worms I bought when I was in Alabama but I knew eventually I was going to run out of those so I did some tentative experimenting and found the seven-inch Berkley Power Worm in the tequila sunrise color was my favorite. I decided not to go any further so I wouldn't get in over my head. I was impressed with my self-control.

This last winter I bought a couple hundred sinking worms in watermelon candy, a few packs of worms in only a couple colors for the Doug rig and a hundred pack of Berkley Power Worms in tequila sunrise. I impressed myself with my restraint. My wife was impressed too. She didn't think I could do it.

As I am finishing this story, Opening Day for bass fishing is only a few days away. I think I'm all set for the season. Over the winter I was rummaging around the basement and found some of those Do Nothing worms from long ago. I might have to give those a try this summer and one of my fishing buddies is talking about a new technique with jigs and plastic crawdads. This might not turn out well. I know how far this can go.

THE HEART OF WHAT MATTERS

My fishing buddy, Mike Hallas has been beating the odds for most of his life. He came from a family with a history of heart problems. His father and uncle both died from heart attacks before either of them reached the age of fifty. Mike knew early on he had heart problems too. He was diagnosed with heart disease when he was a young man in his twenties.

He has been my friend and fishing buddy for the last eighteen years. I met Mike at Gander Mountain. I worked for them for several years after I retired from the Army and Mike was coming into Gander Mountain to conduct hunter safety instruction for young men and the occasional young lady seeking their first hunting license.

Although Mike has always been interested in guns, he himself doesn't hunt. I asked him once why he was doing hunter safety classes when he doesn't hunt and he told me he thought it was important young people know about gun safety and there were few instructors so he volunteered to teach the course. He eventually ended up teaching a hunter and gun safety course every month for a couple years.

I saw him at Gander Mountain when he came in to set

up for his classes and we talked. That lead to meeting for lunch one day in Keys Café in Woodbury, Minnesota which is a favorite for both of us. The people who work there are wonderful and the food is always great. I had lunch there for most of the time I worked at Gander Mountain. As we got to know each other I found out Mike was retired from the Army Reserve so we had a military connection as well. I'm not sure how it first came up in conversation but Mike said something about wanting to go fishing so I invited him to join me one day.

The first lake we fished together was Butternut Lake in western Wisconsin's Polk County on a warm late summer day with a touch of fall in the air. We used the trolling motor as soon as we left the landing. We were fishing over a sizeable weed bed, flipping ChatterBaits over the top of the weeds as fish came charging out to slam our baits. My favorite color is white and it is easy to see the ChatterBait in the clear water. We saw the bait bounce as a fish hit it and we set the hook. Sometimes the bait disappeared and we knew a fish had just inhaled it. We also picked up a couple large northern pike on the ChatterBaits. Later in the day we moved to the other side of the lake where deep water butted up to a rocky shore. Here we switched to sinking worms, fished wacky style. We caught a dozen and a half fish that day and this lake became a favorite of ours.

Looking at the map one day we noticed a smaller lake, Little Butternut just a few miles down the road so one hot summer morning we had to fish that one too. We started with Chatterbaits as we worked around the lake catching a few bass and northern pike. Then we found unusually deep water and switched to crankbaits. After ten- or fifteen-minutes Mike pulled back on his spinning rod and it was doubled over, rod tip plunging as a fish raced off, pulling line off the drag. After a couple of runs Mike got the fish coming toward the boat where I netted it. The fish was a seventeen-inch bass.

Mike went with me on the Mississippi River in the early spring and late fall for walleyes and sauger. It was cold now with occasional snow and frosty winds blasting down the river channel. Sometimes ice formed in the rod guides. One morning Mike had one of the strangest occurrences I'd ever seen. He pulled back to set the hook and his rod was bent as a fish raced off. I dropped my spinning rod and reached for the net. By this time, I could see in the murky water he had a sauger on the line. I extended the net, he led the fish into the net as I pulled up, dragging the fish into the boat. I reached into the net and as I lifted the fish out, I saw six inches of the line with the jig hanging below the fish. As I looked closer, I saw the line was wrapped around the fish. Somehow, I suppose as he was jigging, a loop developed in the line lassoing the fish. In a lifetime of fishing, I never saw that before.

He joined me on my annual Lake of the Woods ice fishing trip we make every February. It is usually a major expedition which includes my son-in-law Damien Aguilar and a friend of Damien's. We would be gone for a long four-day weekend, taking a day to get to the resort, two days of fishing and a day for us to drive back home. In the morning the resort drove us out to our heated ice house just as the sun was coming up on the eastern shore, spreading light across the ice and then in late afternoon back to the resort as the sun sank into the western shore with darkness crawling across the lake.

Eventually, Mike began carrying oxygen with him, making sure to tell me which pocket had his heart medication.

The last few years we put a bet on who catches the biggest fish. There is lots of down time sitting in the ice house starring at floats in ice holes so the bet generates a bit more excitement. We all chipped in five dollars for the person catching the biggest walleye of the trip.

It was late afternoon after a long dry spell when Mike quickly bent over, grabbing one of his ice rods. His float was sinking in the ice hole. It was half the way down the ice hole when Mike yanked up on his ice rod, setting the hook. His rod was doubled over and Mike said "it's a big fish." By the way his ice rod was bent and the time it took for him to get the fish we saw it was going to be a big fish. Damien knelt down next to the ice hole and as a large brown fish filled the ice hole with its head out of water, Damien reached over, grabbed the fish, pulling it out of the water and dropping it on the floor. The fish was twenty-two inches long. Lake of the Woods has a slot limit requiring any walleye nineteen and half inches to twenty-eight inches to be released. We had to release the fish after a quick photo but Mike had the big fish of the fish so far for the trip. When the day ended Mike still had the big fish of the day but we still had another day of fishing left. We fished hard the second day and between the two days we had enough fish for our last night fish fry with a few fish to take back home. But no one caught a bigger fish so Mike got five dollars from all of us plus bragging rights until next years the ice fishing trip.

It was mid-June and Mike and I were going bass fishing for the first time of the summer at one of our favorite lakes, Deer Lake in Wisconsin's Polk County. I heard his car drive into my driveway. I got up, grabbed my coffee cup and walked out of the kitchen through the garage but I didn't see Mike. As I stepped around the back of my wife's car to where Mike parked his car, I saw him standing at the back of his car. His body was shaking and jerking. It was obvious his medical situation had gotten much worse. "I'm going to be ok," he said. "I just got to let everything get caught up." I helped Mike to the side of my vehicle and opened the door. "Don't worry about anything,' I told him. "I'll get the boat hooked up." He hung onto the door as I got the boat hooked up, the shaking stopped and we pulled out of the driveway.

We stopped at a little bar and grill on the way to the lake for breakfast. As we walked into the bar, I saw Mike's knees begin to buckle. I dropped everything in my hands, grabbing him and yelling for the bartender to help me. The bartender was a short, thin young lady probably in her early twenties. She couldn't do much to help me but she did get a bar stool under him and we lowered him onto the stool. Two guys from the café came out by that time and someone called 911. Mike assured us all he was going to be alright but he had to speak to the 911 operator to stop her from sending an ambulance.

He finally got into the café, we ate breakfast and got back in my vehicle. On the way to the lake, I told Mike he had a wear a life vest as long as he was in the boat. He agreed. We went fishing and we caught about four dozen bass. It was a good day of fishing. He didn't have any more difficulties but before I let him drive home, he assured me he was ok to drive. "I never get dizzy when I am sitting," he told me.

A couple weeks later I got a call one evening from Mary Carroll. She is a waitress at Keys Café and after all the years eating there a friend as well. She told me Mike collapsed as he and his wife, Judy were leaving Keys Café after finishing lunch. Mike's heart was giving him more and more problems. Even Mike recognized it and he and his wife got him an appointment at the University of Minnesota heart hospital. They told him he needed a new heart and placed him on the heart transplant list.

Shortly after that my wife Becky and I met Mike and Judy at Keys Café for lunch on a Wednesday. They told us he was going to be on the transplant list for two years and hopefully they were going to find a heart for him. However, Mike is a big man and they needed to find a bigger heart to replace his heart because all hearts aren't the same size.

It was early afternoon the following Saturday when the phone rang. It was Mike on his cell phone on the way to the hospital. They had a heart for him. It was a miracle to find a heart within less than two weeks after getting on the list. There are those who die before a compatible heart can be found for them. I wished him good luck and told him I would say a prayer for him. "It's in God's hands now," Mike said as we ended our phone call. The next day Judy called. The surgical team operated all night to transplant the heart but once it was in place it started beating immediately. Thanks to the grace of God and the skill of his surgical team Mike had once again beaten the odds.

I visited him in the hospital. He was recovering and there were lots of tests to be done and more rehab before he was able to come home. Shortly after coming home, Mike and Judy met Becky and I at Keys Café for his first lunch outside the hospital or his home since his heart transplant. Mary was waiting for us. It was a celebration amongst friends. That began a twice a month tradition for the four of us to meet for lunch at Keys Café. We followed his progress. He couldn't drive for a long time and he had a lot more tests, blood draws and rehab. He missed the ice fishing trip to Lake of the Woods that winter. He got a virus from his new heart and was back in the hospital. He had to take IV medication at home. There were more tests and therapy and finally in very late spring he was able to drive again. He still had to wait when he stood up so everything in his body would stabilize. The doctor told him there was nothing they could do about the dizziness and he just had to be careful.

If he could now drive, could he go fishing. "Sure," the doctor said so we selected a date for the next week. It had been a year since we last fished together. It was time to go fishing again. We kept it like we did before. Mike would bring drinks and snacks. I would have the boat and all the fishing gear ready. Mike also bought his own inflatable life vest. The weather forecast was even encouraging. No rain it said but it would be cool and expect stiff winds. Not bad for a day returning to fishing after a year off.

I was sipping a cup of coffee and reading the morning newspaper when I heard Mike's car in our driveway. Grabbing my coffee, I went out through the garage and Mike had the back of his car open, gathering the clothes he was going to take. I reached into his car, grabbed the ice chest and set it in the back of my vehicle. Mike didn't shake this time and we both knew everything was going to be alright.

We went back to the same bar and grill we went to a year earlier. Mike got out of my vehicle, waited for a minute or two until everything was in balance and then slowly walked into the back door of the bar. We walked around the back of the bar where Mike had collapsed a year ago but this time, he walked slowly but confidently into the café, sitting down at a table against the window where we usually ate. We ordered all meat omelets with toast and coffee. A few minutes later it came and we ate with gusto. Everything was going fine.

At the landing I set the ice chest in the back of the boat, and readied the boat for launch. Mike put on his life vest. It was new enough to still have the sale tag on it. The boat slipped off the trailer once I backed it in the water and Mike holding the bow rope pulled the boat to the dock as I drove the trailer out of the water to parked my vehicle. Mike got in the boat without a problem, took his normal seat in the rear of the boat and I turned the key and the motor rumbled into life. This was an exciting day. My fishing buddy and I were going fishing and last year, with its ups and downs, challenges, surgery, medical procedures and tests, was finally behind us.

I sped across the lake to the north shore where I felt reasonable sure I could find fish. Pulling back on the throttle the boat glided slowly across the water as I put up the back casting chair for Mike and got a rod out for him. Dropping into the front seat, I turned on the depth finder and the trolling motor as I was reaching for my spinning rod. We were fishing.

Mike's first fish was a little ten-inch bass. It wasn't photo worthy. Five minutes later he pulled back on his spinning rod. There was a bend in the rod and the tip was bouncing. Line sliced through the water and in front a fish splashed on the surface. A minute later he had the fish next to the boat and reaching over, he lifted the fish into the boat. It was a fat fourteen-inch fish. That was a better fish so I took his photo before he released the fish.

From there we continued to get strikes and catch fish. Bass bolted out of the water as we fought them. Fished raced off as they doubled over spinning rods. Occasionally a spinning reel drag would whine as a fish pulled line off the reel. Fish swirled on the top of the water and then dove for the bottom. We could see the bass in the clear water as they came closer to the boat and they never gave up. Each one fought hard and some we missed but more often we caught them. We had several doubles where we each caught a fish at the same time.

We fought the wind and eventually moved to the south end of the lake where we were a bit out of the wind. Here we found the fish holding tight to docks and boat lifts. We dropped our baits close to docks and we felt a bump on the line or sometimes saw the line just moving away. Not every dock or boat lift held a fish but enough of them did and we continued to catch fish.

It was late afternoon when we moved to another bay in an effort to get out of the wind. Here we found fish in deep water. Sometimes we only felt weight on the line when we set the hook. Mike cast out and his sinking plastic worm slowly drifted to the bottom. A fish hit subtly but it was enough for him to set the hook and once again feel a bass charge away. Mike caught a bass on his last cast.

At the boat landing Mike backed up the trailer so I could run the boat up on the trailer and he crawled out on the tongue to hook up the safety chain and winch cable. It has been a good day of fishing. We guessed we caught about seventy fish, mostly bass with a few rock bass and bluegill. It was a great day for Mike's first fishing trip with a new heart.

On the way back I asked him if he thought he would be ready for our trip to Lake of the Woods in February. "I think so," he told me. "I think so."

ROMANCE, ADVENTURES AND FISHING

My wife and I got married in a blizzard. It was mid-February and Becky and I exchanged our vows on a stormy night in Oshkosh, Wisconsin. The weather did not dampen the enthusiasm or energy of the wedding reception which followed. The next morning Becky and I drove back to our apartment in Minneapolis. It was a glorious, bright day with fields covered in a fresh blanket of snow, sparkling in the sunlight.

The next morning it was dark as a friend drove us to the airport which took us to Cancun, Mexico, for our honeymoon. Several hours later we landed to bright sun, green palm trees swaying in the wind and a humid, hot day which was such a change from the snow and cold we left behind in the northern Mid West. It was the first time in the tropics for both of us. Our adventure began.

Now thirty years later, Becky and I flew into Fort Lauderdale, Florida to celebrate our anniversary at nearby Pompano Beach. It was dark, chilly and damp when we left our home in Hudson, Wisconsin and warm and sunny when we landed in Florida. One of the advantages of getting married in the winter is it provides a good excuse to go someplace warm to celebrate anniversaries.

Our honeymoon in Cancun was the beginning of our adventures. Fishing adventures too. We loved the warm weather, salty breezes off the ocean and the decadence of being at an all-inclusive resort. The food was great and the drinks were free but every afternoon we took the bus to downtown Cancun and found ourselves ending our afternoon at the same little cantina right across from the bus stop. The beer was always cold and it was pleasant sitting there near the shopping district.

We bought a set of leather luggage and thirty years later we still have one of the pieces. I bought Becky a gold bracelet and we just enjoyed walking around and checking out the little shops and always ended back at the cantina for a quick beer or two before racing across the street to catch the bus to take us back to the resort.

It may have been while we were at the cantina when Becky said to me "we need to go fishing." Neither of us had ever fished the ocean before and it seemed like there was no better time to do that than now. The next day we checked with the tour person at the front desk about scheduling a fishing trip. She took care of it all and a day later we were taking the bus to the docks. Although not sure we were in the right place or at the right boat we trusted the directions we were given. Because we weren't sure of anything we arrived early.

We weren't the only ones questioning if we were at the right spot. Six of us were standing there when the captain finally arrived and confirmed we were at the right place with the right boat. We all crawled on the boat and a couple younger men dragged coolers on board and the motors were started, rumbling to life as the ropes were loosened and the boat pulled away from the dock. The rest of the other fishermen crawled under the overhanging deck of the boat to get into the shade but Becky and I took seats in the back of the boat where the sun hit us. We were going to get as much of the sun as we could before we returned to the snow and ice back home.

The boat slowly motored through a channel, stopping once to pick up a couple older men. They turned out to be the mates for the days fishing. We finally came out of the channel and the boat turned into the ocean. It was a relatively quiet day on the ocean although Becky and I, not sure about sea sickness, had taken Dramamine before we left the resort.

We motored out into the ocean for about half an hour before the boat slowed down and the mates started putting out lines. I was sitting in the fighting chair at the back of the boat and Becky was sitting on a bench on the side of the boat. The mates were distributing bottles of beer from the ice chest. They were brown bottles of Mexican beer, wet from the ice and deliciously cold on a hot day on the ocean.

We were slowly trolling for about half an hour when one of the mates raced over to one of the rods, pulled it out of a rod holder on the side of the boat. There was lots of Spanish being yelled back and forth between the mate and the captain. Becky suggested we might be in the way and should move. As I was getting out of the fighting chair, the mate pointed for me to stay in the chair. As I sat back down, he sunk the butt of the rod in a rod holder between my legs and motioned to me to start reeling.

I felt great weight on the end of the line as the fish pulled back, fighting against the pool cue size fishing rod. A few times it pulled away, taking line off the reel but each time I turned the fish and was getting it closer. It seemed to take forever until I got the fish just below the surface of the water, next to the boat.

There was lots of Spanish being yelled back and forth between the mate and the captain again and the mate pulled out a long gaff hook, leaned over and with all his strength pulled the fish into the boat. He told me it was an amberjack and it looked to weigh about thirty pounds.

Everybody on the boat had the chance to fish, rotating from one to another as the afternoon went on. When it was Becky's turn, she caught a three-foot-long barracuda. The fish put up a strong fight, similar to a northern pike from back in the Mid West but the barracuda fought harder. Everyone had a second chance to catch a fish and when my time came around, I also caught a three-foot-long barracuda. By the time we turned back toward shore everyone caught two fish.

Back at the dock the mate laid the fish out and photos were taken. Becky took a photo of me holding my big amberjack. That photo and one of Becky taken on a warm, soft Mexican night while wearing a bright yellow dress with a straw hat we got at the Cancun shopping center sits on my desk thirty years later.

The adventures continued. Over the next thirty years, Becky and I traveled the world together. There were many more trips to Mexico and other places warm during the winter. We fell in love with Key West, Florida, making it almost a second home for us. We traveled often to Europe. We went first so Becky could see the places I talked about while living almost ten years in Germany during my Army career. We branched out to other European countries on other travels and although we liked it all, our two favorite places in Europe were Garmisch in the Bavarian Alps and Paris.

We continued to fish. Becky caught a seventy-inch sailfish in Key West. We caught peacock bass in Panama. She would be with me when I caught my dream fish, a marlin in Costa Rico. She became my fishing buddy as we fished all over our home state of Wisconsin. In a column I write, I call her The Bass Queen. She has become famous for that and every now and then someone will ask her with a bit of reverence "are you The Bass Queen?"

The sun came out of the Atlantic Ocean, coloring the sky and sea a slick, gun metal gray. It was early in the morning as I stood on the balcony of our hotel room in Pompano Beach. It had been thirty years since the first deep sea fishing trip on our honeymoon. Now we were going fishing again.

"We need to go fishing," Becky said as she searched around, finding a head-boat charter, also referred to as party-boats or drift-boats. These are larger boats taking groups of twenty or more fishermen out on the ocean. They provide licenses, fishing equipment for those who didn't bring their own and bait for a relatively inexpensive charge, usually for a four-hour morning or afternoon charter.

We waited a bit late in our trip to schedule this trip and when she checked on the weather forecast the next day was the only descent weather. Storms with high winds were coming in the next couple days after that. We took the morning charter. It was all set; another fishing trip, another adventure.

Although winds were supposed to be light, we didn't take any chances, gobbling down Dramamine with our breakfast to prevent sea sickness. We added Bailys Irish Cream liquor to our coffee. Why not? We are on vacation and going fishing. It seemed like a great way to start the day.

We took an Uber to the marina. It was already busy with people lined up with their fishing equipment, coolers and back packs waiting to get on the boat. Our boat was called Fish City Pride. It is seventy-one feet long and looked like our group consisted of a couple dozen fishermen of all ages, several women including Becky and a couple kids. There was lots of energy in the group, fishermen chatting with each other, tales of other fishing trips, jokes and laughter and a shared sense of anticipation. What else would we expect from a group getting ready to go fishing.

There was a light wind off the ocean and in the early morning it was cool, justifying our wearing long sleeve t-shirts to start the day. The boat captain signaled for us to get on board and we all moved to the starboard side of the boat where there were benches for us to sit on. One of the mates handed Becky and I heavy casting rod and reel combos. We were going to be fishing in deep water so there was a heavy sinker on each line.

We pulled away from the dock, motoring down the Intracoastal Waterway leading us out into the Atlantic

Ocean. Next to me was a guy named Chuck from Michigan, probably close to my age, mid 70s. He had fished this boat before and caught fish; a good testimonial. Next to him is a dark bearded young man with the daughter of a friend of his. The young girl was probably about six and she had on big white plastic boots. She is all set to catch fish. She tells us this is her second fishing trip and on her first trip she caught only one fish. So, she wasn't skunked.

The boat headed into the ocean and both Chuck and I remark the ocean is as calm as either of us have seen it. The big question, neither of us mention, is if the wind will pick up as the morning goes on. We are out on the ocean for about fifteen minutes when the boat stops and everyone starts dropping lines overboard. We are fishing deep water and I let the casting reel free spool until the sinker hits the bottom. I lock the reel, raise the bait up about a foot, waiting for a strike.

It didn't take long for someone to catch a fish. There is a sense of community with the fishermen on the boat. As the morning went on, anytime someone caught a fish everyone took interest and once the fish came flying into the boat there was a cheer from other fishermen.

The sun is trying to break through the clouds but is not successful. It is nothing more than a white ball, its reflection dances across the top of a light gray sea. In the distance we see other boats cutting across the water silhouetted against the horizon.

There is a jolt on my line and I miss the fish. I now know what a strike feels like and will be ready for the next one. Becky asks me if she will know when she gets a strike and I tell her she will know. For freshwater fisherman it takes a little getting used to. We normally set the hook when we get a strike by pulling back on our fishing rod. You can't do that when fishing deep water in the ocean. Between the depth of the water and stretch in the fishing line you never get a solid hook set so you just start reeling as fast as you can.

We move to another spot and everyone drops their baits down. A few minutes later I feel a sharp jolt again and this time I start reeling as fast as I can. The fish fights back but about half way up from the bottom I no longer feel the fish fighting back and wonder if I lost it but a moment later, I see the fish coming through the water. I swing the fish into the boat. The mate yells it is a red snapper, about fourteen inches long and is a good eating fish so I have a keeper.

My neighbor Chuck misses two fish. Chuck starts to reel in fast and the tip of his heavy fishing rod is bouncing a bit and he pulls in a long white and black fish, almost eel like. I have never seen one before. He tells me last time he was out he caught one and the mate identifies the fish as a sharksucker. This one is about twenty inches long and definitely not a keeper type fish. It is immediately tossed back.

The young girl next to us catches a fish. She is very happy with her fish and now announces she has caught as many fish on this trip as she did on her last trip.

For bait we are using cut up chunks of fish. The mate comes by and with scissors cuts up a couple bait fish, putting the chunks in a small metal try in front of us.

The man with the young girl, starts reeling in his line. The line is slicing through the water. He hands the rod to the young girl and she cranks in a porgy. She now has twice as many fish as she caught on her first fishing trip.

I catch another snapper, a little smaller than the first one but still another keeper fish. We are surrounded by pelicans and sea gulls and they are diving around us trying to catch pieces of bait or fish we throw back. One of the pelicans dips below the surface, grabs Becky's bait and attempts to run off with it. The mate comes running over, pulls the line in hand over hand until the pelican is in, unhooks it and sends it back up in the air. Apparently, this happens on a fairly regular basis so the mate knows exactly what to do.

Becky has learned to drop her bait quickly to keep it away from the pelicans and seagulls and shortly thereafter she starts rapidly cranking on her reel. "I have a fish," she yells and a minute later we see a fish coming through the water. She pulls it in the boat. It is a member of the porgy family and a keeper. She no longer is skunked and very happy with her fish.

We move often, staying in one spot not much longer than fifteen or twenty minutes. Everyone seems to be catching fish. It is a wide assortment of fish brought into the boat. The sun breaks through the gray cloud cover from time to time and we see blue skies and the water turns blue. Once a cloud covers the sun the sea turns gray again.

I feel a strike and start reeling but half way up to the surface I lose it. It is a minor disappointment. No one likes to lose a fish. Another couple moves and half an hour later, I have another strike and this time I get the fish to the side of the boat and pull it in. It is another porgy and a keeper fish.

We get talking to the mate. His name is Jason and he asks us where we are from. We tell him Wisconsin. "Squeaky cheese," he says. It took me a minute to figure out what he was referring to; cheese curds provide a squeaky sound when you eat them fresh. Jason once lived in Chicago and tells us he often drove to Wisconsin to get squeaky cheese.

Finally, the captain announced our last stop. It was getting close to noon and the sun was starting to come out again, starting to get warm. Neither Becky or I had another bite and we reeled up our lines as the boat was starting to turnback toward land. We gave our fish to my neighbor Chuck since he was staying in a condo and could cook them. We had no place to cook fish in our motel.

Once we got back to the docks, the captain dumped all the fish out on cement slab next to the fish cleaning table. There was a good-sized pile of fish. I was glad I wasn't going to clean fish.

Our deep seas fishing adventure came to an end. We went back to our motel and walked a couple blocks to a small restaurant on the beach for lunch. They had a fish dip to die for.

The fishing trip was over and it was a good way to celebrate our thirty years together, remembering our first deep sea fishing trip which started it all. But perhaps the best part was knowing there will be more adventures to come. Love is sharing life's adventures.

OPENING DAY

The most anticipated date on the calendar, as I was growing up, was Opening Day of Wisconsin's fishing season. It certainly eclipsed my birthday and even Christmas. The buildup and anticipation of Opening Day was more exciting than any holiday on the calendar.

For most of my youth and early adulthood Opening Day was the beginning of trout fishing season. In those days, trout season began with the opening of the regular fishing season in May and closed on the last day in September. From the end of trout season to Opening Day, with winter in the middle, seemed like a long time.

As I recall, most Opening Days in my early years fell on Mother's Day. My Mother was fairly patient with Father and me, never objecting to our being absent on that weekend. Years later when I returned to Wisconsin in the early 1990s Opening Day had switched to the first weekend in May, eliminating any conflict of interest over Mother's Day. Apparently, mothers in Wisconsin made it known Opening Day needed to be changed to another weekend.

Once April came along it was just a bit over a month

until the beginning of trout season. Winter was over for the most part, although there was the occasional April snow storm. I got some of the fishing bug satisfied with a few evening fishing trips to the Fox River for walleyes but it wasn't trout fishing. The days seemed to move in slow motion toward Opening Day. When we were a couple weeks out, the fever really set in as Father and I started serious planning for our Opening Day weekend expedition. A couple days out we started packing the car.

We had our traditions. Mother would make us a baked chicken and blueberry pie for Friday night, the day before Opening Day. We drove north to Dunbar staying in a motel. They had small kitchens in a couple rooms and Father made sure he reserved one of them for us. We left Friday afternoon once I got out of school. While traveling we stopped at a rest area and ate the chicken and the first slices of the blueberry pie. Once we got to the motel and dragged everything into the room, we got out the fishing gear. Waders, creels, fishing vests were placed in the trunk. We tied on hooks and pinched on sinkers to our lines. Although using fly rods, we bait fished with night crawlers. Our target was brook trout and the Woods Creek was a fairly small stream so live bait was our preferred and most productive method of fishing. The rods were also set out in the trunk. We streamlined our preparations so there was little time lost and no chance of forgetting anything the next morning.

Sleeping the night before was a bit fretful. I dreamt of all the fish I was going to catch. However, the ringing of the alarm clock always jolted me awake. It was dark outside and most often there was frost on the car windows. Dad made eggs and bacon with toast and coffee. The room came alive with the smell of bacon and to this day, now over half a century later, I still associate the smell of bacon with going fishing. While he was making breakfast I packed the ice chest with a beer for him, soda for me, a couple sandwiches and of course our night crawlers. It was on these trips Father let me drink coffee. We finished breakfast, and headed out the door with another cup of coffee to drink as we drove to the stream.

The excitement was just about as much as I could stand then. It seemed to take forever to get to the stream as night started turning gray with daylight coming. Finally, we rumbled over the bridge which crossed the Woods Creek and Father pulled the car off to the side of the road. It didn't take long to pull on waders, slip into fishing vests, drape nets and creels over shoulders, join fly rods together, slam the trunk and start walking down the dirt road which ran parallel to the stream. Father would go in first and I continued on to the end of the road, slipped into the woods heading for the stream. As I walked further into the woods, I could hear the stream trickling and gurgling over the rocks. It has been half a century or so since those days but I still remember what a lovely sound it was. Then I was lowering myself off the bank and into the stream with the water creeping up the sides of the waders, tugging at my legs. There wasn't a better feeling anywhere in the world than standing in the middle of the Woods Creek as I was getting ready to make my first cast of the new season.

All Opening Days were special but there are two which especially stand out in my memories. One was my last opening day before joining the Army. It had been a wet spring and when I slid into the stream, I noticed the water was higher and faster than I ever saw it before. I put an extra split shot on my line to get the bait to the bottom. The first brookie I caught was an eleven-inch fish. For a stream like the Woods Creek, it was a good-sized trout. A little later my bait drifted under an overhanging tree, branches brushing the surface of the water. I felt a fish slam my bait and when I set the hook the water exploded. I luckily got the fish out from under the tree and into the main current. It put up a great fight and a moment or two later I slipped the net under it. It was a fourteen-inch brook trout. For the Woods Creek this was a trophy. By the time I finished my run in the late morning I had a limit of trout ranging from eleven to fourteen inches. Fishing on the Woods Creek was always good but never this good. I couldn't wait to show these fish to Father. He met me back at the car and dumping out his creel, his trout went from eleven to fourteen inches as well. We had identical limits of trout. It had been an awesome Opening Day.

I didn't realize it then but I was about three months way from joining the Army and leaving for Basic Training at Fort Leonard Wood, Missouri and shortly after that on my way to Germany. Three years later I returned to Wisconsin, fresh out of the Army, going back to school with the GI Bill to get a degree and a commission in the Army. I was a week away from graduation and becoming a second lieutenant when Father and I and now my kid brother David, on his first trip to the Woods Creek, left for Opening Day.

All the same excitement came back to me. The morning drive to the stream still seemed to take forever and then we were there, rushing to get our gear on and the three of us walking down the gravel road. Father went in the woods first and David and I walked to the end of the road before cutting into the woods. The excitement was there as we got closer to the stream, hearing the rushing water, sliding off the bank into the water.

David missed his first fish and he was greatly disappointed but I told him not to worry; there would be more than enough fish before the morning was over. We got to one of my favorite pools and on his first cast he had a fish on. He seemed a bit peeved when I didn't get the net out fast enough. By late morning we both had our limit of brook trout and were walking back to the car. We saw Father through the barren spring woods and David yelled to him "we have our limits." David took a great deal of pride in that. I was proud too to be a part of it as well.

A week later I graduated from college, pinned on the gold bar of a second lieutenant and left for Officer Basic Course at Fort McLellan, Alabama. That was my last Opening Day on the Woods Creek.

In the years after there were two more tours to Germany, assignments in Alabama and North Carolina and a deployment to Desert Storm before I would return to the Mid West. After retiring from the Army, I bought a home in Hudson Wisconsin. A number of things had changed. My enthusiasm for trout had waned, replaced with a passion for bass fishing and pleasantly surprised to find some of the best bass fishing in the country in northwest Wisconsin. Father had gotten older too by then and although he still trout fished, continuing to wade the streams, he had begun to slow down. He stopped going out on Opening Day saying there were too many people on the streams and his first trout fishing trip in the new season would be sometime in the middle of the week after Opening Day when he had the stream to himself.

I invited him to join me on Opening Day for bass fishing. He liked that and it became our new Opening Day tradition. There was some of that old Opening Day excitement again for us. I remember the Friday night before Opening Day when I was in the garage making sure the boat and all the gear was ready for the next day. It was just like when I was a kid. Everything needed to be ready so all we had to do was have breakfast, make a quick lunch, hook up the boat and we could be gone without any unnecessary wasted time or forgetting anything. He came out with me in the garage and we talked about those Opening Days of the past as I was working on the boat, checking gear, and making sure the trolling motor battery was charged. We both still felt the thrill of Opening Day.

Our Opening Days were a bit different. We didn't wake up before dawn, now preferring to get out about midmorning. I made breakfast before we left and then making sandwiches for us, putting water and four beers in the ice chest. His favorite beer was Special Export and we had one with lunch and then the other one when we took a short break in the middle of the afternoon.

Once again, we were going fishing on Opening Day. "I got one," Father would yell and I looked over to see his rod tip plunging, spinning rod bent in half as a bass raced off. We had another five more Opening Days before he passed away.

After Father was gone, my wife Becky became my Opening Day buddy over the last twenty years. We developed our own Opening Day traditions. We talk about Opening

Day for much of April. There are several long discussions as to which lake to fish on Opening Day. We reminisced about Opening Days passed. For the week prior to Opening Day, I am getting rods and tackle boxes ready. The gas tank on the boat is filled and trolling motor charged. For me, getting ready for Opening Day is part of the excitement. The night before we usually order pizza so we did not have to worry about cooking the night before. We just want to relax, savor the moment and enjoy the anticipation.

There is no frenzy to get up early. We get up when we wake, hook the boat up and stop at a bar and grill for breakfast on the way to the lake. My wife is mainly a fair-weather fisherperson. Cold and rain is not her thing and she doesn't see any reason to be uncomfortable while fishing. However, she makes an exception for Opening Day. Regardless of the weather she goes out on Opening Day with me. We have had some unpleasant weather that first Saturday in May. There has been rain and sleet and wind and cold temperatures but she still goes out with me to feel the rush when the first bass of the season hits the bait. We also have had some unusually warm weather. A couple times in the last few years we fished in t-shirts on Opening Day.

Success has been spotty over the years. Early May can be a tough time to catch bass. The last couple years, after some brutally long winters followed by cold wet springs, has been especially challenging. Last year, Becky caught two fish within five minutes in the early part of the day. I had only a strike for several hours of fishing. It was a larger lake and we fished better than half the lake before I pick up two bass in back-to-back casts at the end of a point in the last half hour. Those four fish were the only ones we caught.

The year before we fished a smaller lake because some of the lakes still had ice on them midweek when I drove north to check on the condition of the lakes before Opening Day. We selected this smaller lake since it was one of the few completely ice free. The day was bright but cold and windy. We fished hard and I caught one small ten-inch bass and a fifteen-inch northern pike. Becky didn't have a strike until the last few minutes before we were going to leave when she caught a foot long bass.

We had other days when the fish were hitting. On one of those warm Opening Days, we were in t-shirts by early afternoon. I heard Becky yell from the back of the boat and looking over I saw her spinning rod doubled over and heard the drag on the reel giving out line. "Big fish," she shouted. I brought in my line, dropped the rod on the floor of the front casting deck and stepping down to the floor I grabbed the net. The water was clear and as I looked down, I saw a large shadow below. The fish made several runs before Becky started getting the fish closer to the boat. I could now see it and the fish was a large northern pike. She led the fish into the net and I pulled it into the boat. The fish was about fifteen pounds and was the biggest northern pike she ever caught. On that day we caught another two dozen bass. It was one of our best Opening Days.

Over the last few years, I have noticed changes to Opening Day and I'm not sure why. There just doesn't seem to be the same thrill and excitement by fishermen as there once was for Opening Day. For me the excitement hasn't changed in over fifty years but for a lot of others the enthusiasm has died. I can remember the first twelve or fifteen years after moving to northwestern Wisconsin when boat landings were packed on Opening Day. At one small lake near our home, the parking lot was usually packed and other fishermen parked their cars and boat trailers on the road off the landing. I see fewer people at boat landings and fewer fishermen on the lakes now than I ever remembered.

We have friends, Ron and Pat Stager who own Deer Lake Sports on Highway 8 in northwestern Wisconsin. Becky and I normally stop to see them after we leave the lake on Opening Day. Last year we mentioned to Pat we were surprised to see so few fishermen on the lake. She told us she just doesn't see the excitement Opening Day once had either. They have owned the bait and sport shop for over twenty-five years and she told us in the first few years they started getting people coming in for bait the day before Opening Day and it continued through Sunday morning. "We had the shop opened and worked for over thirty hours straight," she said. "Now, we don't get many fishermen coming in for Opening Day."

There are more changes for Opening Day now. The inland trout season, when trout may be kept, begins the first Saturday in May and closes the middle of October. There also is now a catch and release season with only artificial bait for trout beginning on the first Saturday in January running through the Friday before the season opens for fishermen to keep trout. Bass fishing has changed this year with publication of new regulations. Opening Day for bass is now when fish may be kept with the rest of the year open for catch and release fishing.

I'm not sure how to feel about the new seasons. As far as bass fishing is concerned, it seems since most of my fishing is catch and release fishing anyway, there essentially is no more

Opening Day. I will miss the excitement and anticipation for Opening Day. I always looked forward to that day and although Opening Day, as I know it, may be gone I will always have the memories and what memories they are.

GIRLS GO FISHING

"Girls need to go fishing too," my oldest daughter Lisa told me when she had her first daughter and our first granddaughter.

Now that daughter, Amelia is fifteen years old and she and her sister Abigail, soon to turn thirteen are visiting Grandpa and Grandma in northwestern Wisconsin, for a few days, so we have to go fishing.

The night before Amelia and Abbigail help load the boat. They take the panfish rods they were going to use from the basement out to the garage along with the panfish box. We use winter ice jigs on spincasting rods, placing floats or bobbers as I call them, about three feet above the jig. For bait we use wax worms.

Wax worms tend to be difficult to find in summer. I don't know why. They are perfect baits all year long for bluegill. A number of bait shops in our area think wax worms are good only in winter. When in doubt about where to find wax worms, Grandma called Deer Lake Sports located east of St Croix Falls right on Highway 8. She talked to Ron and Pat. "Don't worry," they told her. "We'll have a tub of them waiting for you."

It is going to be a hot summer day so we decide to start a bit earlier. It didn't take long to get the girls going once I woke them. I remember many years ago waking their mother and her sister, their aunt, up early when they were young to go fishing. It didn't take them long to get going either. There is something about fishing which does that. Getting them up for school was a different matter.

My wife Becky, their grandmother and I are getting water and ice in ice chests along with the other things we needed. Once the girls are standing in the kitchen, Grandma sent them out to the garage to help me drag the boat out. I am on one side of the boat and the girls are on the other side, pulling the boat out to our vehicle, helping me hook it up. We are ready. We add the ice chests to the boat, pile in our vehicle and roll out of the driveway.

Today Grandma and I are introducing the girls to the time-honored fishing tradition of stopping for breakfast at one of the cafes on the way to the lake. It just wouldn't be quite the same; going fishing without stopping for breakfast. It would be almost like forgetting the bait. We stop at the Not Justa Bar and Grill on Highway 35 near Somerset. Amelia and Abigail order waffles, Grandma has a breakfast sandwich with hash browns and Grandpa got corn beef hash with eggs.

It is cool and quiet in the café and we must have been hungry or in a hurry to go fishing because it didn't take long for everyone to eat, use the rest room and get back out to the vehicle. Temperatures are beginning to heat up outside.

Half an hour later we stop at Deer Lake Sport Shop. The girls are introduced to Ron and Pat, Amelia gave Ron and Pat's dog Schmidty dog treats and the girls inspected the wax worms. Over the years the girls have become a good judge of wax worms. Only the "juiciest" looking wax worms will do and they approve of the tub of wax worms.

Twenty minutes later, after taking the straps off the boat and spraying on sunscreen I am backing the boat and trailer into the lake. Grandma and the girls are in the boat and as soon as it floats off the trailer Grandma starts the motor, pulling away from shore. I park the vehicle and walk out on the dock where Grandma and the girls pick me up. I point across the lake to a shore lined with brush and submerged trees. "Our fish will be there," I tell them.

As we pull up to the brushy shore, I drop the trolling motor while the girls get their spincasting rods out. It doesn't take long to bait hooks and both girls cast their lines out. Within a minute the first bobber begins to bounce and Abigail pulls in the first fish, a small bluegill. Although it is a small fish it bent the spincasting rod, rod tip bouncing with fish splashing on the surface.

It is windy and I try fighting the wind with the trolling motor. The wind is pushing us along fairly quickly. We are moving too fast and not getting enough time to fish good looking spots. I find a tree toppled into the water, branches protruding through the surface. There should be lots of bluegills here so I drop anchor.

The girls are steadily catching fish. Some are small and some are big. They are all fun to catch and there is much laughing and giggling as fish are splashing next to the boat. We lost count of how many times both girls had fish on at the same time. Grandma insures everyone is drinking enough water. It is getting hotter as the day goes on and luckily it is windy, otherwise it would be a real scorcher.

This spot begins to slow down so we pull anchor and with the trolling motor move long the bank. The girls pick up a few more fish and then we pull into a more protected stretch of shoreline with a knocked down tree and lots of shade over the water. We drop anchor again. Immediately bluegills begin hitting.

Amelia set the hook as her bobber dips below the surface and her spincasting rod is bent in half. This is a bigger fish than what they have been catching. Within a few moments we see why. Amelia brings a foot long bass to the side of the boat. We caught a couple smaller, six-inch bass earlier but this is the first good size bass we catch.

A couple minutes later Abigail's rod is bucking and her fish is running sideways and, in the water, we see a thin black shape. It is crappie and once she pulls it in the boat, I am amazed how black it is. It is black crappie and during the spawn and a couple a weeks after, they turn almost black before returning to their normal color.

It is early afternoon and we are hot and tired. The girls caught and released about a hundred panfish, mostly bluegills along with about a dozen crappie and a few bass.

On the way back we stop at a drive-in and get some burgers and chicken nuggets to eat on the way home. Once we get home Grandma takes the girls to our neighbor's swimming pool to cool off. What a day it has been.

There is something special about taking kids fishing. It is heartwarming to watch their enthusiasm catching fish, even small fish. There is a simple pleasure in watching a bobber and how exciting it is when that bobber sinks in the water as a fish hits. Then there is a bend in the rod and a tug on line and essentially this is what fishing is all about. To see and feel the true essence of fishing, take a kid fishing.

And oh yah, girls got to go fishing too.

WHAT IS THERE NOT TO LOVE ABOUT WHITE BASS?

My first big fishing adventure was fishing with my grandfather for white bass. I heard Grandpa talk for years about fishing all night in the spring on the Fox and Wolf Rivers for white bass and the great numbers of fish they caught. I couldn't wait to join him. My parents might not have been as enthused about my staying up all night to fish but eventually they relented. I was somewhere around thirteen or fourteen years old at the time and had fished with Grandpa on Lake Winnebago but never all night on the Fox River.

When I finally got their permission and Grandpa was willing to take me out with him on this great fishing trip, I was all keyed up for a week. This was now bigtime fishing. It was on a Friday night when he drove over from his home in Sheboygan to pick me up. I was finally going to go. We launched at a park in Oshkosh. It still was light but the sun was quickly disappearing as we moved upriver. We passed under the Highway 41 Bridge and Grandpa motored off to the side, a bit up from the bridge. I dropped the anchor as Grandpa turned off the motor.

Grandpa set up the boat. He wanted everything just right and organized once it got dark when the fish started hitting. He wanted nothing to interfere with our catching fish. In between us he placed the minnow bucket and an empty five-gallon bucket. The five-gallon bucket was for us to throw our fish in. Then he hung a lantern over the side of boat. He had an iron S hook with the bottom inserted in the oar bracket and the lantern about three feet above the boat with the light shining on the inside of the boat and on the water on the outside. By this time there were other boats and it was now dark and their lights shined around us. On the bridge I saw cars crossing the river, their lights stabbing into the night. Occasionally we heard some talking from some of the other boats but for the most part it was fairly quiet except for the sound of the hissing of the lantern and the rushing of the river around us. It has been almost sixty years since that first fishing trip on the river with Grandpa but I can still remember the sound of the river.

It didn't take long before we started getting strikes. Or at least to me it seemed that way then. We fished Wolf River Rigs with minnows. The sinkers were probably about three quarters ounce and it was enough weight to get the bait to the bottom. Grandpa taught me to drop the rig until the sinker hit the bottom and then bring it up six inches so the bait rode just above the bottom.

When the fish hit, they struck fast and hard. I had a small fiberglass spincasting rod and as soon as the rod tip began to bounce, I set the hook. My light rod was doubled over as the fish surged off and it bucked as I cranked on the

Johnson Century spincasting reel until finally the fish was splashing alongside the boat and I hauled it in. Twisting the hook out, I dropped the fish in the bucket, baited the hook again and lowered it back in the water. I didn't want to waste any time getting the bait back in the water.

The schools of fish came and went. There were times between strikes when I could eat a sandwich or have a cup of hot chocolate. But when the white bass were hitting it was wild. At times, we both had fish on at the same time. In the early hours of the morning when the fishing slowed down, I would occasionally nod off but the next strike had me wide awake again.

On this first trip the white bass had just started with a few late run walleyes so the two runs sort of over lapped. On this trip we were catching walleyes as well as white bass but white bass were the largest number of fish we caught. I caught a couple four-pound catfish, which for a young fisherman were trophy fish.

Finally, the horizon started to turn gray as light took over the sky. It was time to go home. Grandpa turned off the lantern and pulled it in while I pulled up the anchor. It had been a wild night of fishing on the river. Our bucket was three quarters full of fish, mainly white bass, a few walleyes and my two trophy catfish. Grandpa dropped me off at home and I went to bed exhausted. As I slept, I saw the rod tip bouncing in my dreams as a fish hit. From then on, I have always liked white bass.

White bass have a lot going for them. They are found mainly in rivers or lakes with rivers running through them. When they are found they normally are in huge schools where you can catch a bunch of them at a time. Contrary to some popular beliefs, they are good to eat. But best of all they put up a hard fight when caught.

Some people think white bass are in the same family with largemouth and smallmouth bass which are actually part of the sunfish family so they are lumped in with panfish. White bass are separate and in the temperate bass family which includes yellow bass as well. The yellow bass seem to be far and few between. I'm not sure I ever caught one but I caught lots of white bass.

The white bass run on the Fox and Wolf Rivers is legendary, drawing fishermen from throughout the Mid West. I recently saw a photo taken in the early 1900s of a bunch of fishermen lined shoulder to shoulder across a railroad bridge in Oshkosh, fishing for white bass in the spring. Probably the Indians, living along the river before white men showed up, took part in the spring white bass run too.

The white bass would start moving up the Fox River from Lake Winnebago sometime in April depending on the weather. If we were having a warm spring they would start in early April and if it was cold, it could be toward the end of the month. Many old timers would say the best time in the spring for white bass was when trees were in bloom. The run usually lasted through May and sometimes even into early June. For a few weeks in June white bass and walleyes could be taken trolling Floating Rapalas in the lake outside the mouth of the Fox River.

It was the Friday before Memorial Day weekend. My wife Becky and I were back in Oshkosh visiting family. We dragged the boat back to Oshkosh to get in the last of the white bass run. After launching at the same park where Grandpa and I launched many years ago, we motored upriver to the Highway 41 Bridge. We started working our way along the rip rap casting quarter ounce pink and silver spinners. It was a warm, bright day with little wind.

We worked from the north end of the bridge going south on the western side. We caught nothing. That seemed strange to me. We went under the bridge where the main part of the river ran and worked our way back north on the eastern side. Again nothing. I was beginning to think perhaps we had missed the last of the white bass run. It had been a couple hours and we didn't have a strike.

We eventually decided to move to the southern end of the bridge. On the eastern side the water is shallow and weedy. We went under the bridge where there is a break in the rip rap and the road runs only a few feet above the water. As we came through it to the western side, my line tightened as a fish raced off. My ultralight spinning rod was doubled over and the rod tip was plunging. The fish even managed to take some line off the reel by the time I got it splashing next to the boat. It was a fat, three-pound white bass. A couple casts later Becky got a white bass as big as the one I just released. We found the fish. In the next hour and a half, we caught fish, it seemed, every few casts and we lost count of how many fish we caught and released that afternoon.

The next day we returned to the same spot. The weather had changed drastically. It now was cold and windy with gray clouds shifting overhead. We were wearing a lot more shirts and jackets now. We started where we caught fish the day before. Now nothing. The fish had definitely moved out. We worked up and down the bridge on both sides. Again nothing. I switched from the spinner we used the day before to a jig and eventually caught two walleyes but we never saw another white bass. I guess we did hit the end of the white bass run.

I now live close to the Mississippi River and although the white bass run here doesn't reach the fabled traditions of the run on the Fox and Wolf Rivers, the Mississippi does have a major springtime run of white bass. These fish come up from Lake Pepin and I find them at the dam north of Red Wing, Minnesota. One of the other differences is that although we catch a few white bass throughout the spring the heavy concentration of white bass doesn't show up until usually sometime in the last half of April and they seem to be around for only a week or two before they disappear back into Lake Pepin.

My fishing buddy, Dale Good and I were on the Mississippi River shortly after the middle of April. It was a cool, overcast day with the hint of rain. Our plan was to fish for white bass for a while to see if there were any in the river yet and then switch to walleyes for the rest of the day. We were casting quarter ounce firetiger blade spoons. There is a rocky island which separates the lock from the dam and we fished on the dam side, flipping our baits toward the rocky bank.

In less than two or three casts we had the first fish. It struck hard, pulling away, rod bent in half, line slicing thru the water. In the next four hours the fishing was fast and furious. We lost count of the times we both had fish on at the same time. It never stopped all day long. We never went more than four or five casts without a strike. We took a quick break for a sandwich and then started again. The fish continued to strike. Even by white bass standards it was incredible fishing. By the end of the afternoon when we finally headed the boat downriver back to the landing, we estimated we caught well over a hundred fish. Most of the fish ran from two to three pounds. The fishing for white bass was so good we didn't miss fishing for walleyes. A week later I returned and the white bass were gone.

Many people consider white bass a spring time fish but they can be caught all year long. Summer can be a particularly good time for white bass and the first time I encountered that was with my grandfather on a hot, summer day. It was one of those days when the water looked dark blue and the sky a light blue with few clouds, light winds just ruffling the surface and a bright, hot summer sun shining down. It was relatively early in the morning and everything seemed fresh with the excitement of fishing on a perfect day for a fourteen old boy.

We motored out on Lake Winnebago and after a bit Grandpa shut off the motor and told me to drop the anchor. Fishing with him was like that. I have no idea as to how he picked where we fished but it seemed it didn't matter because we always caught fish. Mind you, those where the days before depth finders/fish finders. Fishing started slow. We picked up about a half dozen white bass and they went into the fish backet that hung over the side of the boat. Grandpa never discriminated against white bass. He kept and ate whatever fish he caught. He once told me if white bass were as tough to catch as walleyes more people would probably appreciate them.

We were out for probably about an hour and a half when Grandpa thinking out loud, suggested it might be time to move further out to find some walleyes. Within minutes of his saying that it was like a someone flipped a switch. It was a surge as we hit a massive school of white bass. We both were using two rods but it quickly became apparent we couldn't keep up. We dropped our bait to the bottom and immediately a white bass slammed it. The fish fought hard and my little fiberglass spincasting rod was constantly bouncing as a fish raced off. The fish continued attacking our minnows. The action was so fast that we didn't even take time to put the fish in the fish basked, instead just throwing them down onto the floor of the boat. Within an hour we were out of minnows. I dug into my tackle box and found a jar of Uncle Josh white pork strips. I threaded one on the hook of my Wolf River Rig, dropped it down, jigged it up and down for a moment or two and a white bass hit it. Actually, the pork strips worked better than minnows since it stayed on the hook better. I continued to get a strike every time I dropped my bait to the bottom.

Grandpa was now picking up fish and putting them in the basket as I kept catching fish and throwing them on the floor. Finally, he put a stop to it, telling me we had more than enough fish. The fish basket was way over half full. It had been one of the most incredible fishing experiences of my young life up to that point.

Thirty years later I renewed my enthusiasm for summer white bass fishing. I and my family returned from our last tour to Germany and were back in Oshkosh on leave for the month of July. My son, Todd was fourteen at the time, the same age I had been on that fantastic day when Grandpa and I ran into that huge school of white bass on

Winnebago. Two or three times a week I took him fishing in the evenings, fishing off the rip rap on the Highway 41 Bridge.

I drove as far as I could into the grass on the north end of the bridge and we walked down the rest of the way to a small break in the bridge where the water came thru. From the rocks we cast small chartreuse spinners and silver Kastmaster spoons. We didn't hit any huge schools of white bass but we usually managed to cast a dozen or more white bass each night as well as the occasional walleye.

White bass hadn't changed much since I last remembered them from the days of my youth. They hit hard, putting up a tenacious fight. It was starting to get dark as Todd and I walked back to the car with our stringer of fish. On the way back to my parent's house where we were staying, I drove over to the southside of Oshkosh, stopping at Ardy & Ed's for a root beer in an icy mug. It was a great way to end the evening. A few nights later I made white bass fillets on the grill. It made for a wonderful summer dinner.

Although not nearly as pronounced as in the spring there always seemed to be a surge in white bass action in the fall again. Shortly after I retired from the Army and moved to Hudson, Wisconsin, my son, now sixteen, and I fished Cedar Lake in St. Croix County. It was the first Saturday in November and the first time we fished that lake and didn't know what to expect or what fish were in the lake.

The day was over cast and cold with just a hint of wind. We started with silver Floating Rapalas. We fished for over an hour and hadn't got a strike yet when suddenly Todd pulled back on his spinning rod to set the hook. The fish took off and a minute later he pulled a fat chunky white bass into the boat. We fished the area for another half an hour and didn't get another hit. That seemed strange to me since normally when you catch one white bass you can expect to catch more.

We switched to ultralight spinning rods and the same pink and white spinner my wife Becky and I had done so well earlier in the spring at the Highway 41 Bridge at Oshkosh. I moved the boat into shallower water and we started casting toward the rocky shore. Within a few minutes we had another white bass. We continued along the shore line and steadily got strikes. There seemed to be a school of white bass and we followed them down the lake.

They just hammered our baits, bolting off, doubling over our ultralight spinning rods and occasionally pulled line off the reel as they charged off. The next couple hours were incredible and we lost count of how many white bass we caught and released. I had one fish which swallowed the treble hook and I tore the fish up trying to get the hook out. I hated to release it, knowing it was just going to die. A few minutes later I saw a lady raking leaves on her lawn and I yelled over to her if she would like a white bass. She yelled back "I sure would" so I pulled the boat up on the beach in front of her house and threw the fish up on the lawn. She raced over, picked it and waved to us. Another person who likes to eat white bass. By late afternoon the fishing slowed down and we headed home. We guessed we caught well over three dozen bass that afternoon. I went back to Cedar Lake in spring when I thought it would be a no brainer to find white bass and never caught another one in that lake again. Apparently white bass can be finicky at times.

I have always loved to catch white bass from the first

time I fished for them as a young boy with my grandfather on the Fox River. Still today, I look forward to finding a school of white bass on the Mississippi River or where ever I find them. They hit hard, put up a strong fight and can be found all year long. They are good to eat too. What is there not to love about white bass.

WHITE BASS ON THE GRILL

Scale white bass, leaving the skin on before filleting. Leaving the skin on keeps the fillets together as they are grilled. Soak the fillets in milk for at least an hour. Take fillets out of the milk, rinse off with water and pat dry with paper toweling.

Light the grill. Either charcoal or propane gas grills will work. Cover the grill with aluminum foil and punch holes in aluminum foil with a knife to let the smoke out. There are fine mesh grills that can be placed on top of the normal grill and those work well instead of aluminum foil.

Mix melted butter and Worcestershire Sauce half and half in a small pan and place on the side of the grill to keep warm. Place fillets on grill. Turn fillets often and each time baste with melted butter and Worcestershire Sauce.

Cook until fillets are brown on the edges. Remove from grill and serve. Salt and pepper to taste. Enjoy.

THE NATURE OF MUSKIE FISHING

There is fishing and then there is muskie fishing. Fishing for most freshwater species is completely different than muskie fishing. There is nothing else like it.

To start with, the chances of success is considerably less than for any other fish. Not catching a muskie seems to be the norm. Seeing a muskie or raising a fish as muskie fishermen call it is downright exciting and is considered a successful day. The odds against not catching a muskie are fairly good. But when you actually have a muskie hit and see the water explode as you set the hook, drag screaming as the fish runs off, heavy casting rod bent in half, praying everything goes right and then finally getting a fish longer than your leg to the side of the boat you know there is nothing in freshwater fishing which compares to the heart pounding excitement of actually catching a muskie.

Perhaps it is the challenge, and maybe if you are lucky enough the sheer thrill of catching the toughest and most elusive fish in the lake, which keeps fishermen coming back time and again, regardless of the outcome.

It was on a week in mid October when Nate and Brenda

Dennis flew in from their home in Oregon to join my wife Becky and me for a long weekend on a muskie lake in northern Wisconsin. The lake is Sand Lake about a dozen miles from Hayward. Hayward bills itself as the Muskie Capital of the World and if you are going to be in the Hayward area you might as well go muskie fishing. In the middle of this time my wife turned sixty-five years old which was another good reason to spend a long weekend at a cabin in Wisconsin's Northwoods.

She told me she chose this cabin on this lake because it has muskies and she expected Nate and I to go muskie fishing. She and Brenda planned on sitting next to the fireplace, keeping the fire going, and just relaxing; thank you.

The logistics for this venture were fairly extensive. Coronavirus cases were increasing significantly throughout Wisconsin to include the north country so we weren't going to restaurants or bars and grills. We had to take everything we needed for the next five days. The morning we left, we packed five plastic boxes and four ice chests with food and drinks and loaded them in the back of our boat. We certainly were going to eat and drink well regardless if the muskies were hitting or not. For muskie gear I took a soft sided tackle bag of muskie baits and three casting rods.

We drove the three hours north to the cabin from our home in Hudson and got there as the sun was starting to slip toward the western horizon. We unloaded the boat and our vehicle, dragged everything in the cabin and then went looking for the boat landing.

The boat landing was on the other side of the lake from the cabin. Nate and I launched the boat and Becky and Brenda drove our vehicle and boat trailer back to the cabin as Nate and I motored across the lake to the cabin. It was overcast and cold with light winds. By the time we found the cabin from the lake side it was starting to get dark but it looked like we had an hour of daylight left.

We put on more clothes and I grabbed the muskie tackle box as we headed down the steps to the dock where the boat was tied to. We motored east of the cabin to a point where weeds sprung up out of the water. Whenever you get on a new lake there is always the question of where you will find fish. With muskies it is even worse. You never know where to start so I just picked a likely spot with deeper water close to weeds. We moved around with the motor until I found ten to twelve feet of water. Looks as good as any spot I thought to myself as I turned off the motor.

On both of our lines I put on my favorite muskie bait; a one and an eighth ounce black spinnerbait with orange spinner blades. I have caught more muskies on this bait than any other in the tackle bag. By his own admission Nate hadn't used a casting outfit for a couple decades. I handed him the rod and although his first couple casts were a bit short within a few minutes he was casting like he had been doing it all his life.

It was cold so we both put on gloves as we worked along the weed line and then along the shore. Finally, it was dark and we put away the rods and turned the outboard back on, skimming across the water to the dock. We hadn't gotten a strike but that was ok. We looked at the last hour as mere practice, getting us ready for the rest of the weekend. As we climbed the stairs back uphill toward the cabin, I smelled wood smoke. Becky and Brenda had a fire going. It felt good to get into the cabin, leaving the cold behind as the warmth greeted us. Today had been a good start. We got to the cabin safely, set ourselves up for the next several days, had a good fire going in the fireplace and more chances to catch a muskie in the days to come.

The next morning, I looked outside when I got out of bed. There was snow on the top of my vehicle. It seemed a bit early for snow but perhaps it might turn the muskies on. It was snowing again as we walked down to the dock. The dock was covered in snow and so was the boat. It was just a gentle snowfall we get so often in the late fall. We bushed the snow off the seats and headed west to another point with weeds extending out into the lake.

We kept fishing with the spinnerbait we used the night before. I have great confidence in it. Our lines arched out into the lake, big spinnerbaits splashing into the water. I looked at the water temperature gauge on my fish finder and it read forty-eight degrees.

Within minutes the wind picked up and so did the snow. Fog rolled in and we could barely make out another boat on the other side of the point. The wind lashed at us, snow beating against our faces. It felt like continuous pin pricks on our skin. I always hate to let the weather beat me but it was painful and unrelenting. I turned the boat around so we could fish with our backs to the wind but we couldn't hold the boat in place. When we went back to fishing into the wind our baits were being thrown back at us, our faces are red and raw and our glasses covered in slush. I tried to wipe the snow off my glasses but within a minute they were full of snow again. I looked toward land. It wasn't that far away but I couldn't see it in the swirling fog and snow. Luckily, I could just barely make out the tops of the trees.

Nate agreed it was useless to stay any longer. We quickly put away the rods and I turned on the motor. I went as fast as I could which wasn't very fast because I couldn't see very far between the snow and fog and slush on my glasses. I was trying to see out of the side of my glasses to keep the tree line in sight. I knew we weren't far from the cabin but it seemed to take forever until I saw the dock loom up in front of us. I don't think I've been happier to see a dock in my life.

We tied off the boat, slipped and slid across the dock and walked carefully up the snow-covered steps to the cabin. We were grateful for the blast of warm air as we pushed open the door. We were soaked and started taking our clothes off in the hallway which also had a washer and dryer. Throwing wet clothes in the dryer, we bolted for our rooms and dry, warm clothes. The coffee was still on and we held coffee cups with both hands trying to warm them up. The coffee needed something more so we poured in a shot of bourbon. It was just right now. Sitting in front of the fireplace, the fire was warming the outer man and the coffee with bourbon was warming the inner man. We had not seen a muskie so it looked like the muskies weren't turned on by the snow. We fisherman weren't either.

The snow finally stopped and the wind dropped but it still was cold and gray as Nate and I went out later in the afternoon. It was quiet on the water with a freshness to the air after the storm. We are still using spinnerbaits and went back to where we fished in the morning. Without the snow pelting us and the wind pushing the boat around it made fishing a lot easier. We worked along the bank, getting into the rhythm of casting, retrieving the bait while watching behind it, looking for a big fish following. We worked our way back to the dock, tied up the boat and looking up we could see the lights looking warm and inviting from the cabin and the smell of wood smoke coming out of the fireplace chimney. Muskies are the fish of ten thousand casts but all it takes is one good cast. Maybe tomorrow. Muskie fishermen must have hope.

The next day was Becky's birthday. She turned 65 and decided to celebrate by visiting the St Croix Rod Store in Park Falls. We drove an hour through the Northwoods to get there. It was overcast with the threat of snow in the air but it wasn't snowing. Becky decided she needed to buy us both a new St. Croix rod for wacky worm fishing. She didn't like the ones we were using. She made the nice young man who helped us feel guilty because they had temporarily suspended factory tours, compounding it by mentioning it was birthday. The young man gave her a baseball cap as a birthday present. Becky bought two six-foot one-piece medium spinning rods. We are all set for next summer. What a way to celebrate a birthday. That is why she is known as The Bass Queen.

Outside of the St Croix Rod Store we see a bait and tackle vending machine. I have seen some bait vending machines before but not one which has tackle too. It has bobbers, hooks, sinkers, spools of fishing line and a few baits in addition to cannisters of live bait. St Croix Rods thinks of everything.

We got back to the cabin in the late afternoon and there was still enough daylight for Nate and I to get in an hour or so of fishing. We pulled on heavy clothes and gloves, grabbed the casting rods and headed for the dock. It was cold and the wind bit into us. By the time it was dark, we had worked our way along the shore back to the dock. We never saw a fish. Muskie fishing seems to be more frustration than success but a bad day of muskie fishing can become a great day of muskie fishing with just one cast. That is what keeps muskie fisherman going.

The next day was Sunday and a Packer Sunday on top of it. We started the morning by my having my World-Famous Sausage Gravy. We poured the gravy over biscuits with fried eggs on top of the gravy. Breakfast was filling and of course we had dark roast coffee, strong enough for the Northwoods followed by a couple courses of Bloody Mary's. It was a great way to start Packer Sunday, lingering over coffee and Bloody Mary's with the Packer game a late afternoon game we found ourselves with about an hour and a half time for muskie fishing.

It was cold and windy. We switched baits. I pulled out my second favorite muskie bait, a black and orange Nils Master bait and put it on Nate's casting rod. I found another orange bait and put that on my line. It was cold. We should be getting used to this by now. We went west of the cabin, fishing in ten to fifteen feet of water. We didn't see any fish again. We flushed a huge flock of Canada Geese and between their honking and splashing as they lifted off the surface of the water they made a lot of racket. On the way back to the cabin we came across two guys dragging sucker minnows for muskies. I asked them if there were muskies in this lake and they confirmed muskies were there but they hadn't had a strike either.

We got back to the cabin in time to mix a drink before kickoff, turned on the electric fireplace in the downstairs level of the cabin and put the game on. At half time Nate and I had a bratwurst but that didn't help. The Packers lost to Tampa Bay. The Packers were having as much luck as we were muskie fishing.

It is the last day. Nate and I will spend most of the day muskie fishing. It is our last chance. We started the morning by finishing off my World-Famous Sausage Gravy with left over biscuits and eggs on top. We had one Bloody Mary for luck. Before we pulled away from the dock, I went through the tackle box and took out two different baits. Today we were going to do some experimenting with baits. As we were leaving the dock, I thought I felt snow against my face. Half way across the lake the snow picked up. But there was little wind so the snow was no more than a light blizzard. We planned on fishing the other side of the lake we hadn't fished yet. We started fishing deep water off a rocky point. That kind of spot has always been one of my favorite spots for bass so it might work for muskies too. It didn't.

We changed baits and worked the weedy edge of the rocky bank which stretched across that side of the lake. In the quiet water leaves scattered by the wind floated on the surface. The snow continued to fall and it remained cold. Even with gloves our hands were cold. The afternoon wore on and we continued casting, occasionally changing baits, looking for the right one.

It was late afternoon and with the overcast day there wasn't much light left. We went back near our cabin. We switched baits again and this would now be our last stand.

It got darker as we fished. Finally, we just had to give in. We had given it our best shot. The next morning, we are leaving and before it gets too dark Nate and I needed to put the boat back on the trailer so we are ready to leave after we pack, load the boxes and ice chests back in the boat and clean the cabin tomorrow morning. I drop Nate back at the dock for him to get our vehicle and boat trailer and drive over to the landing as I head across the lake to meet him. It gave me a few moments to reflect on the last few days.

Had we failed to catch a muskie? I think not. Muskie fishing is a sport loaded with frustration and long days without catching a fish. This is not a failure. It is merely success delayed. If we have hope and continue to dream of catching a muskie and keep fishing for them, then we know it is just a matter of time before some day we will see that long shadow trailing behind our bait before it finally hits.

The next morning, we pack and load everything back in the boat and our vehicle. There is an early fall blizzard blowing in so we want to leave as soon as we can. However, we drive into Hayward to show Nate a real muskie. We stop at the Moccasin Bar and Nate and I go in to see Cal Johnson's sixty-seven-pound, eight-ounce world record muskie caught on July 24, 1949. It was caught on an artificial bait probably not much different than the ones Nate and I were fishing. Nate looks at the fish with awe. "That's one big fish," we both say. Regardless if it is a record or not, catching a muskie takes just one cast. It is the nature of muskie fishing.

MIKE YURK'S WORLD-FAMOUS SAUSAGE GRAVY AND BISCUITS

On this muskie fishing trip I made a double batch of my World-Famous Sausage Gravy. It was enough for four of us to have on two mornings at the cabin for Becky's birthday bash in the Northwoods before muskie fishing on cold and snowy mid October days.

Two pounds of bulk pork or breakfast sausage
One large onion
Two packets of packaged country or sausage gravy mix (my favorite is
McCormick although any of the white gravy mixes found in any grocery store
will work just fine)
Two cups of milk
Two cups of water
One can of biscuits per meal
Eggs

Place bulk sausage in a pan turned to medium high heat, break up the sausage into small pieces as it is frying. Peel and dice the onion. Once the sausage is starting to brown add the onions and continue to brown until sausage is somewhat crunchy.

As the sausage is browning, dump water and milk into a pot on medium heat and add the gravy mix, stir regularly until gravy begins to boil, reduce heat to a simmer and add the sausage and onions.

While the gravy is cooking, put the biscuits in the oven.

The oven should be preheated to 350 and bake biscuits for about fifteen minutes.

To serve-break biscuits in half, pour sausage gravy over them, add fried eggs on top and serve to hungry muskie fishermen and/or Packer fans and their wives.

Enjoy.

A SUMMER STORM

"Get off the lake," Diane yelled at Becky. "There is a storm coming your way."

It had been a pleasant summer day and my wife Becky and I were fishing Deer Lake, one of our favorite lakes in Polk County. It was bright and sunny with light winds. Temperatures were in the seventies. We caught a bunch of bass. It was a good day of fishing with wonderful weather.

Now it was late afternoon when we returned to the boat landing. Becky dropped me off at the dock to back in the boat trailer. She motored out in front of the dock and was circling around in front of the landing as I was walking across the parking lot to back the trailer into the water. She picked up her cell phone and called our friend Diane to see if she and her husband Marty were going to Friday night fish fry.

Diane asked where we were and Becky told her Deer Lake. Diane told her to get off the lake quickly. Becky looked around and saw nothing which looked like a storm. We still had blue, sunny skies. Becky told me about her phone call as we tied down the boat on the trailer and got everything put away for the drive home.

We drove up the hill from the boat landing to the main road. Once on the main road, we saw dark clouds building up in the western sky. As we drove south, we watched as nasty looking clouds march across the sky. The day become darker as we drove.

"I guess Diane was right," I said. "It looks like there is a storm behind us." As we drove further south, skies to the north of us were getting darker by the minute.

"We did get off at the right time," Becky said. "But we didn't see anything while we were on the lake."

The storm was moving fast and it was getting uglier as we drove. To the south skies were still bright and clear. A light rain began to fall and by the time we got to our home in Hudson the clear skies were gone and it was getting dark with rain splattering down.

Early next morning I woke and went downstairs to the kitchen to turn on the coffee maker. It was still raining and the skies were dark. My fishing buddy, Doug Hurd and I planned to go fishing. Neither of us usually relish going out in the rain but sometimes you need to fish when you can despite the weather. Becky checked the weather for me and said it was possible for the weather to break in a bit so we used that as justification not to cancel our fishing plans. By the time we drove north and had breakfast perhaps the weather would be better. That was what we hoped for as we headed back to Polk County.

The further north we drove the darker the skies became as rain drummed on top of my vehicle. We were still hoping for the break in the weather. As we drove past Magnor Lake in the western edge of Polk County we saw a tree blown down, blocking the landing. This was not looking good. Just a couple hundred yards away from the landing on the other side of the road is a convenience store/gas station/ restaurant where we planned to have breakfast. As we pulled into the parking lot, we noticed the building was dark. Everything was closed. There were a couple other trucks in the parking lot with guys standing outside their trucks despite the rain. We got out and walked over.

"There is no power anywhere around here," one man told us. We looked around and saw the cabins and houses around Magnor Lake were dark and without power too.

"That was one hell of a storm last night," the other man said. "There were straight line winds over a hundred miles an hour."

This was not looking good but as Doug and I got back in the truck we weren't ready to give up yet but this called for a change in plans. I called another café I knew some twenty miles away in Centuria on the eastern side of the county. Perhaps the storm hadn't been so bad there. A young lady answered the phone and by the noise I heard in the background it sounded like they were busy so they were open. She confirmed they had power in the area around them and open for business.

It continued to rain as we drove to Centuria and as we walked across the café parking lot it seemed as if the rain was beginning to lighten up. This could be good news. The café was packed. We ordered coffee and their special, called the Sunrise Skillet which consists of corn beef hash with a couple basted eggs and melted cheese on top. It a great way to start a fishing trip. We finished breakfast and ordered another pot of coffee. We were hoping to wait out the storm. By the time we finished the rest of the coffee it looked as if the rain was reduced to a light drizzle. This was getting better by the minute.

We decided to fish Half Moon Lake. It was another change in plans since we originally planned on fishing another lake. On the way north we stopped at another town for gas. By the time I paid for the gas the rain had stopped. This was going to be a good day after all.

We pulled into the small park at the lake where the landing is and instantly saw the destruction from the night before. A tree was knocked over, crushing what looked to the frame of what was going to be a big tent for some kind of celebration. On the point just down from the landing, another tree was uprooted with half the trunk and branches in the water. The porta potty was blown over. A mighty storm had come through here.

Doug and I got the boat ready to launch, putting our tackle boxes in the boat, taking the straps off the back of the boat and raising the motor. We were already to back the boat into the water when a light rain began coming down. We were here and we weren't going to let a little rain stop us.

We pulled on rain gear and I crawled into the boat. Doug backed the trailer into the landing, unhooked the winch and the boat slid into the water. As Doug drove out of the landing to park, I started the motor and slowly motored over to the dock, grabbing a dock pole. Doug walked out on the dock and just as he was about to step into the boat a bolt of lightning slashed across gray skies followed by an explosion of thunder.

Doug and I looked at each other and he said "I'm not comfortable with this."

"Ya," I said. "I promised my wife I wasn't going to fish during a lightning storm."

Doug walked back over to my vehicle and backed the trailer into the water. I ran the boat up on the trailer to where Doug could hook up the winch and cranked the boat the rest of the way on the trailer. We put the tackle boxes back in the vehicle, put straps on the back of the boat and dropped the motor. Pulling off our rain gear we got back in the vehicle and drove off on our way back home as the rain came slashing down again. It was storming. This fishing trip just wasn't meant to be.

Summer storms can be fierce. Cold fronts and warm fronts clash, bringing a deluge of rain and strong winds with dark skies split by lightning and the bombardment of thunder. Summers spawn harsh weather, culminating in a fury which tear apart the land, frightening us while reminding us of the power found in nature. This lake had been hit by one of those summer storms.

A week later I called Doug. "We got to go back to Half Moon and make up for our last trip there."."

"You're right," he said.

It was cool with light winds, gray clouds floating overhead as we were driving north to the lake. But it wasn't raining or storming. We looked on this as being a positive development. We stopped at the same café we were at two weeks earlier. We ordered their Sunrise Skillet again. The food was good and it still wasn't raining. Maybe our luck had changed.

At the boat landing we still saw the aftermath of the

storm. Some of it was picked up and the porta potty was upright but the trees were still laying on the ground. It might take time to get them cut up and carted off.

We launched the boat and headed across to the north shore of the lake. The first place we stopped had several cabins and houses with trees knocked over on their lawns, roots yanked from the ground. We stopped for a minute to take in the damage. It must have been one hell of a storm.

The water underneath their docks and boat lifts is shallow and we flipped wacky worms up and around them. On the second dock I felt a light tick and set the hook. The fish tried to run off but it came up splashing on the surface of the water. It was an eleven-inch bass. It was the first bass of the day and we had wondered what the storm, even two weeks later, would do to the fishing.

We caught a few more fish by the time we moved into deeper water further down the shore. Here we could see the fury of the storm. Almost every house seemed to have a tree blown down on the lawn and other trees smashing roofs and porches. Now we also saw some docks and boat lifts twisted and torn from the storm. It was devastating. Some roofs had tarps pulled across holes in the roofs. A couple of the houses had work crews on the roofs replacing shingles. We heard the machine gun like bursts from the nail guns. We could not imagine the heartache some of the owners have. Dream homes and family cabins now in shambles. In some cases, it looked like it was going to be easier to tear down the old building and start over.

We fished Ned Rigs and Drop Shot Rigs in deeper water, picking up a few more fish and they were bigger in the deeper water. As we fished, we were in awe of such power and severity of the storm. It is hard to believe how bad this must have been. Luckily no one we heard of was killed or injured. That in itself was a miracle. Sometimes there are miracles in the worse disasters.

Further down the lake we saw the erratic nature of powerful storms. We now saw two or three cabins and homes without any damage and next to them another one torn apart from the storm and winds. It was breathtaking in an eerie way. Perhaps there were more miracles.

At the end of the lake there was a deep hole close to the bank. The boat house in front of us was crushed but other buildings around it seemed untouched. It was strange and a bit unsettling to see what the storm did.

I switched to a new rig I read about called a Tokyo Rig. It has a wire with a sinker on one end and a hook on the other. I threaded a plastic worm on it and cast out. A couple casts later a fish slammed it. It is always fun to catch a fish on a new method.

At the end of the lake, it was shallow with lots of weeds and lily pads. I switched again to another new method called a swimming jig. It is a bass jig with a plastic trailer and instead of pitching it to structure, it is retrieved like a crankbait. I put on a big brown jig and within a couple minutes a fish jolted my retrieve to a stop as it took off for the weeds. It was a fourteen-inch bass, caught on another new bait.

We turned now to the south side of the lake and saw very little damage from the storm. It was like there were two lakes. One battered by a vicious storm and the other untouched. The inconsistencies are astonishing, bewildering and frightening,

By the end of the day Doug and I caught and released over forty bass so we made up for our last trip but it was bittersweet. Our heart ached for the people who had damage to their property. It was going to take a long time to overcome this storm. It also was frightening to see the brutal power of this storm. Summer storms are always the worst.

THE SEPTEMBER OPEN

Turning off Interstate 35 through the town of Moose Lake on my way north, I pass Moose Horn Lake on the edge of town and aways wondered what fish were there. Normally, I was on my way to Northern Minnesota where I meet a group of guys for the Minnesota fishing season opener or later in the fall for a gathering we call The Fall Classic.

One day when I talked to my fishing buddy Dennis, I told him I keep going by this lake and it looked interesting and some day we need to fish it. With that, we began making plans to fish it in a couple of weeks. In mid-September, a perfect time for a fall fishing, Dennis and I with another fishing buddy, Mike were pushing my boat off into the water of Moose Horn Lake. We stopped a few minutes earlier at a local bait shop and the guy behind the counter didn't sound real encouraging when we asked if there were in bass in the lake. He mumbled something about there might be some bass there but he really didn't know.

We weren't going to let a bit of negativity stop us as we motored across the lake, stopping short of a large weed bed which seemed to circle the lake. We put white ChatterBaits on our spinning rods, running them over the weeds. Within minutes, fish raced out of the weeds, attacking our baits, doubling over spinning rods and occasionally making the reels whine as they pulled line off the drag.

Most of the fish were northern pike ranging from twenty to twenty-five inches in length but there were also bass. At the end of the day, we had over three dozen northerns and another eight largemouth bass. All the bass ranged from twelve to fifteen inches. It was a glorious fall day with good weather, cooler in the morning, warming up with bright sun, highlighting the brilliant fall colors on the trees and best of all, great fishing.

A year later, Dennis and Mike and I returned. Again, it was cool in the morning before the sun burned off the dampness. We were drifting past the now abandoned-for-the-season swimming beach. A fish slammed my ChatterBait, rocketed for the surface where it swirled on top before racing off again. It was a tough fight by the time I got the fish next to the boat where Mike netted it for me. The fish was a fourteen-inch smallmouth bass. It was a pleasant surprise since we hadn't caught any smallies the year before but in some ways wasn't a surprise since the Moose Horn River ran through the lake.

As I was pulling my fish out of the net to remove the hook and release it, Mike picked up his spinning rod, which he set aside to net my fish. His bait was still in the water and as he tightened the line, his rod tip began to bounce. He yelled he had a fish too and a couple moments later I extended the net for him, pulling in another smallmouth bass, the same size as mine. It was a most extraordinary catch.

That was the beginning of what we call The September Open. More people began joining us over the years. We made a couple deviations from our normal plan of fishing Moose Horn Lake. One year we fished a lake closer to Duluth because one member of the group owned part of island in the lake and he bragged about the walleyes there. We did catch walleyes and perch but it seemed it bit too far to go.

Another year we heard of lake not far from Moose Lake, again which reportedly had walleyes in it. We only caught one walleye on that trip but got a bunch of perch. Another year, one of the regulars of The September Open, Ryan got permission from his father-in-law to let us use the family cabin on a lake west of the Twin Cities. We fished the lake the afternoon and evening we arrived and the next morning; catching bass and northern pike with Ryan catching big fish with a nineteen-inch bass.

With those exceptions we continued to go to Moose Horn Lake for The September Open. After several years, we inexplicability began to catch fewer fish. We didn't know why. We were using the same baits which always worked but now catching fewer fish. We consulted a map book and found another nearby lake called Sand Lake. We weren't ready yet to abandon Moose Horn Lake so we stuck with it in the morning and when we realized the fishing wasn't getting any better, we moved in the afternoon to Sand Lake. There we found more bass and northern pike.

It became inevitable when we eventually did give up on Moose Horn Lake. It just wasn't producing fish. It was a shame since it was the lake which initially drew us up there to start with and became such a part of the legacy of The

September Open. Instead, we switched completely to Sand Lake and it is large enough to handle several boats and still have good fishing.

Last year, to start, there were nine of us; Scott, Doug, Mike, Joe another Scott with his two sons Parker and Avery, Dennis and me. Ryan and Vinnie meet us at the landing for lunch later in the morning.

As part of our September Open routine, we meet in the parking lot of a Fleet Farm off the interstate. Once we are all accounted for and people are shifted to other vehicles for the ride to the lake we leave, stopping enroute at a café in Pine City for breakfast. Breakfast is the typical gathering of fishermen, excited about going fishing. Between cups of coffee there are memories shared of previous September Opens, bragging about new fishing gear, and discussions on weather and how good the fishing will be today. One measure of how good a café is how fast they can serve breakfast. After all we are going fishing and can't waste a lot of time eating. Our breakfast is typical fare; eggs, bacon, omelets, toast brought to us quickly so we are soon back on the road. We have a convoy with boats. The sun is out as we leave and the day is starting to warm up.

Mike is riding with me. I hadn't realized it had been a year since the last September Open when we had seen each other. We cover all the basics, he telling me how he and his family are doing and I tell him how my wife and I have been in the last year. I tell him of my travels since we last saw each other and, of course, we talk about fishing. The hour goes by fast as we drive north, watching the landscape change from farm fields and hardwood trees starting to change color interspersed with bright green pines. We pull in to the landing and there is the typical frenzy of everyone putting last minute stuff in boats, launching and parking vehicles.

Mike and I drift away from the dock as I start the motor. In front of the landing is a large bay leading us to the main lake. At a far eastern corner of the main lake is another long bay and Mike and I head for it. As often as we have fished this lake no one has ever fished that bay. We are excited at the possibilities as we pull into it. New water can do that to fishermen. It looks perfect. Lots of docks and boat lifts jutting out in the lake. The water seems to be a little shallow but we think it shouldn't matter.

We start with wacky worms, flipping then into the docks and under boat lifts. We fish for some time without a strike. We are perplexed. We should have fish by this time. As we were wondering what is happening, Mike pulls his spinning rod up and the rod tip is bouncing as a fish takes off. A moment or two later Mike pulls a foot long bass into the boat. That is the first encouraging sign but after another several more disappointing docks we give up. I tell Mike we should have more fish by now and it is time to find new water. Perhaps the shallow water did matter.

We move back into the main lake and pass Doug and Scott. They have a dozen bass, mostly caught on wacky worms in deep water. Mike and I move down the lake and find deeper water off a large weed bank, switching to ChatterBaits. It takes us a few minutes before Mikes connects on the first fish. It is fourteen-inch largemouth bass. Ten minutes later I cast, let the bait sink for a couple seconds and then start retrieving. A fish slams my bait, line slicing through the water as it charges away. My fish is a twenty-four-inch northern pike. By lunch time Mike and

I have about ten fish, a mixture of bass and northern pike. We can feel the difference in the fish. A bass hits harder and stays deeper. The northern pike hit lighter and after an initial hard fight come closer to the surface, giving up as it gets to the boat.

It is lunch time and all the boats start back to the landing. Ryan and Vinnie meet us on shore where they made lunch. Ryan made lunch on a camp cooker and has it laid out in aluminum pans on a table. He calls it a low country boil and in the pans are shrimp, sausage, potatoes and corn. It is huge treat for all of us who normally are used to sandwiches for lunch. We are sitting in the shade, eating good food with all the banter between friends. There are more stories recalled, recaps of the mornings fishing, jokes and laughter. It seems wacky worms were the most successful baits.

The boats push off from shore for a couple more hours of fishing in the afternoon. Ryan joins Mike and I as we work the shoreline, pitching wacky worms into docks and boat lifts. This part of the lake has deeper water close to shore where the fish are hitting reasonably well and we are catching fish.

Ryan flips his bait to a corner of a dock, lets it sink for a moment and then pulls back hard on his spinning rod. His spinning rod is bent in half as the drag on the reel gives out line. This is a big fish. We are scrambling around the boat, trying to stay out of Ryan's way as he fights the fish. The fish swirls on top of the leaving a ring the size of a wash tub on the surface. I get the net out and wait until Ryan has the fish alongside the boat where he leads it into the net and I pull up, dragging the fish into the boat. It is a huge fish and measures nineteen and a half inches. It seems fitting the cook who provide such a great lunch catches the biggest fish of the trip.

Dennis and Doug come by to tell us they are heading in for the day. Mike, Ryan and I decide to fish for another hour and we are the last boat, from our group, to leave. It is still sunny and warm. It has been a good day. Dennis sums up The September Open best when he told me "with good friends and good food, catching fish is a bonus."

RYAN'S LOW COUNTRY BOIL

4 pounds shrimp
8 ears of corn broken in half
2 to 3 pounds of kielbasa
4 pounds medium red potatoes
3 onions quarters
¾ cup of Old Bay seasoning

Fill a seven-gallon stock pot half way with water. Add seasoning, bring water to a boil and then add potatoes and onions. Bring the water back to a boil for about five minutes. Add kielbasa and bring back to a boil for about fifteen minutes. Add the corn and bring the water back to a boil and cook for ten minutes. Add shrimp, bring water back to a boil until shrimp turn pink.

Drain in a colander, discard water and serve. Enjoy.

BIG WATER, BIG FISH

As we pulled away from the landing, pointing the boat toward open water beyond the breakwater, we were motoring into a rising sun. The eastern sky was bright orange right above the surface of the water and as it rose it turned a lighter shade of orange, reflected on the quiet surface of the waters of Green Bay.

I turned to my buddy Doug and told him I never saw Green Bay this quiet and calm. Doug looked around and agreed. "Me neither," he said. It truly was an anomaly on this first full day of fishing Green Bay.

As we got beyond the breakwater at Oconto, we picked up speed as we raced across the glass like calm of Green Bay, heading toward the mouth of the Peshtigo River. By the time we got to the mouth of the river, the horizon was a band of silver, filtering into a pale blue sky above. The day was still chilly but it held the promise of warmth to it. The water was a darker shade of blue, now with a slight ripple from a breath of wind.

There are three of us fishing Green Bay; Ben Aeilts and

Doug Hurd both from Minnesota and me from Hudson, Wisconsin. We drove across the state of Wisconsin the morning before to Oconto on the western shore of Green Bay. We are here in pursuit of big walleyes.

That first afternoon we launched Ben's 21-foot Skeeter boat into the Oconto River because strong winds were whipping the water of Green Bay into large swells making fishing the bay almost impossible. For the afternoon we fished the river. We never got a strike but our disappointment was tempered by the fact no one else in the other boats, caught anything either. The consensus was the walleyes were not in the river yet, still staging in the bay waiting for the right conditions for them to surge into the river on their way to their spawning areas.

It was late afternoon when the wind began to drop and the bay looked fishable. We motored downriver, passed the breakwater and the mouth of the river, moving around the backside of the breakwater to about ten to twelve feet of water.

We each put on a different bait. I am using a blade spoon, Doug used a Cabela's Rip-N-Glide and Ben fished a Rippin Rap. The waves are still rolling but not as bad as earlier when the wind was much worse.

Half an hour later Ben pulls back on his spinning rod and it is doubled over with the tip plunging. He was lifting his bait off the bottom when a fish hit. The fish puts up a tough fight. There are a couple of short runs but each time Ben turns the fish and finally brings it into the net Doug is extending. It is a heavy fish, fat with eggs. Although we don't measure the fish, we guess it must run about twenty-six to twenty-seven inches. "That's what we are looking for," Ben says as he slips the fish back in the water.

Twenty minutes later Doug yells he has a fish. The fish charges off and Doug stops the run. A few moments later I lift the net up underneath the fish, pulling it in the boat. It is a bit smaller than the first fish but still a very nice fish.

Those were the only two fish we get that evening but both are big fish. The long day of driving and fishing took its toll. We head back to the landing and then to the farm house outside Oconto where we will be staying. It is a small two-story farm house probably built sometime in the first half of the Twentieth Century. As we look around, once we get to the farm house and start putting our gear and food away, it makes one wonder about the families who were here before us, the joys and occasional heart breaks they endured, cooking in the kitchen, sitting around the dining room table eating supper and the life they lived here.

That night I made bratwurst on a grill outside the back of the house. As I stand next to the grill, I heard the yelp of sandhill cranes in the field on the other side of the wood line behind the house. We have coleslaw and potato chips with our bratwurst, slathered in mustard and onions piled on top. It is a typical Wisconsin meal which is so appropriate with the city of Green Bay, Lambeau Field and the Packers only thirty miles south of us.

The next morning there are a number of other boats around the mouth of the Peshtigo River. The sun is up and it is a bright morning with the far shore broken by water and sky shimmering at the end of our sight. Without the wind it is quiet and we hear the guttural honking of Canada geese, the shrill screeches of sea gulls mingled with the songs of red wing black birds and sounds of ducks calling to each other.

Fishing is slow and we see few nets coming out from other boats. All three of us are fishing Rippin Raps made by Rapala in different colors. I start with silver and blue, one of my favorite color combinations. We fish for about an hour, still without a strike. We troll from directly in front of the river to the south of it.

Ben yells he has a fish. He tells us it isn't fighting like a walleye and a couple moments later we see why. It is northern pike. Doug gets the net under the fish, pulling it in the boat. It is about thirty inches long.

A few casts later I am motivated to change colors. After digging around in my tackle bag, I come up with a gold and purple Rippin Rap. Twenty minutes later I feel weight on the end of my line. "I have something," I say. "It might just be a branch." There is no fight to it and it is coming along as just dead weight. Half way back to the boat I feel movement. "Wait a minute," I yell. "It is a fish." Now the fish is pulling back and makes a couple short runs before we see it in the water. It is another northern pike, thirty inches in length. Although it wasn't exactly what we are after it does feel good to have a fish.

Twenty minutes later a fish slams my bait. It races away and my spinning rod is bent in half. It puts up a powerful fight, staying deep. We see the golden-brown color of a walleye, making a huge silhouette in the water. The fish is about two feet long, fat with spawn and lots of muscle. It is my first walleye in Green Bay.

We fish for another half an hour without a strike. Ben suggests we move so we motored back along the shore to a spot halfway between the Peshtigo and Oconto Rivers. Within twenty minutes after stopping, a fish attacked my bait as I was lifting my Rippin Rap off the bottom. The fish was like a rocket, never hesitating. It pulled away, straining line and my spinning rod. I finally stopped the run but the fight was far from over. The fish never gave up, even when I finally got it in the net. It is another two-foot-long walleye. The fish are swollen with spawn so they are much heavier than a normal two-foot-long walleye. I guess the fish was probably in the seven-pound weight. As I unhooked the fish, dropping it back in the water, I proclaimed the gold and purple color my new favorite color. I also point out my last two walleyes are some of the biggest I have caught.

The Bay of Green Bay stretches south from Big Bay de Noc in Michigan for one hundred and eighteen miles to the city of Green Bay. It is twenty-three miles across at the widest point. The city of Green Bay, known for the Green Bay Packers, bratwurst and Friday night perch fries to name just a few of its charms, is on the far southern end of the bay at the mouth of the Fox River. The first white man to explore the Bay of Green Bay was a French explorer, Jean Nicolet. He established a trading post near the site of present-day Green Bay in 1634, making it one of the oldest European settlements in what eventually became America.

The Bay of Green Bay is a piece of big water and is also known for fishing and big fish. Besides huge walleyes and northern pike the bay has muskies, trophy smallmouth bass, as well as salmon and trout since their introduction in the 1960s. It is also legendary for yellow perch. Not only where they once commercially fished in Green Bay but provided great sport fishing. My Grandfather fished Green Bay for perch in the 1930s and told stories of coming home with buckets of them.

In early spring it is also renown throughout the Mid West for big walleyes. At the landing in Oconto there are boats from Illinois, Michigan, Missouri, and Iowa in addition to Wisconsin and Minnesota. Fishing on the bay is featured on several state and regional fishing shows and while we were there, we saw a couple shows being filmed.

In early April the walleyes begin to stage in the bay near the mouths of rivers. Once the water temperature gets into the mid to high 40s these fish start to move into the river to spawn. Before the spawn, these fish will be found in five to fifteen feet of water in the bay. Most of these fish will be big females. If your goal is to catch a thirty-inch walleye, this is the time and place to do that. The Bay of Green Bay is big water for big fish.

In early afternoon the wind picks up, bringing in gray clouds overwhelming the blue, sunny skies. Even the water on the bay turns gray. Doug rummages around his tackle bag and changes to a Cabela's Rip-N-Glide in gold with red spots. A few minutes later he yells "Here's a fish."

I look over to him on the other side of the boat and his spinning rod is bouncing as a fish stays deep, steadily pulling away. The fish hit the bait off the bottom and is still hugging the gravel. I quickly get my bait in, grab the net and stand next to Doug as he fights the fish. It took a few moments for Doug to get the fish off the bottom and ultimately next to the boat. I extend the net but the fish pulls away and Doug has to lead the fish back toward the net. Finally, the head is in the net as I sweep the fish into it, lifting it out of the water. It is another big walleye and our last for the day.

By midafternoon the weather is getting worse. Big water, such as on Green Bay, can change quickly and weather is always a concern. It doesn't take long for everything to change on big water and it is dangerous to ignore.

We end up in front of the breakwater at the mouth of the Oconto. At the end of the breakwater is a pile of ice at least six feet high, washed up on it by wind and waves. There is even a blue tint to it like a glacier. A light rain is beginning to fall and it doesn't take long for us to be wet and cold. No one is catching any fish now. We decide to call it a day.

It is a relief to get inside the breakwater and away from the wind and waves. Once we get the boat back on the trailer and are getting everything ready in the parking lot of the landing to leave, we congratulate ourselves on our timing. The rain has picked up, the wind seems worse and it is getting colder.

We had a good day. We caught and released ten walleyes and the two northern pike which started our day. All of the walleyes are big fish, ranging in size from twenty to twenty-eight inches. In many places, catching just one fish like this is a good day but here big fish are the norm. Green Bay has big water for big fish.

FISHING WITH KIM

She is in her swim suit, long red hair over her shoulder and down her back. She held a cane pole in her hand while standing on the bank of a pond in Alabama. She is four years old.

The bobber dipped and she raised the rod, bent in half as a fish surged off and finally flinging a bluegill (or as they call them down south a bream) in the grass behind her. She had a big smile on her face as I twisted the hook out of the fish, dropping it back in the water and baited her hook with a couple kernels of canned corn.

Her name is Kim and she is my youngest daughter.

We were stationed briefly in Alabama at Fort McClellan while I was going through training before leaving for our second tour to Germany. During that short summer and early fall we were in Alabama, our Sunday family tradition was to fish a small pond on the backside of Fort McClellan. The pond was loaded with bluegill. We usually grilled hot dogs for dinner and after we ate, I got out cane poles I bought at the local Walmart. They were just right for kids.

All they needed was about six to eight feet of line, a small bobber and a hook and a can of corn.

Most of the fish were small but Kim and her sister Lisa didn't care. They loved to see the bobber go down with the tip of the cane pole plunging as the fish pulled away, twisting and fighting and splashing on the surface as they hauled the fish out of the water, flipping them on the bank. We never kept any of the fish as Kim and her sister just liked to catch them.

From Alabama we went to Germany. On a late summer day, I took Kim and Lisa trout fishing at a pond in eastern central Germany. It was a classic fishing trip. The night before we searched for nightcrawlers and the girls reached eagerly into the dirt and grasses for nightcrawlers. I remember doing the same thing the night before fishing when I was a kid.

It was still dark when I got the girls up and they woke quickly and got dressed. Their mother would have been happy to see them move so fast the mornings they went to school. It was just barely light when we got to the pond and everyone grabbed something as we walked around to the far side of the pond to set up. It didn't take long for the first trout to strike.

I watched as a bobber began to dance on the surface of the pond while I handed the rod to Kim. I told her to wait a minute and when the bobber began to sink under the surface, I told her to set the hook. I'm not sure I ever explained to her how to set the hook but she seemed to instinctively understand. The trout bolted for the surface and Kim kept furiously cranking on the reel, rod doubled over as the fish ran off. She finally got the fish to the bank and I netted it for her. It was a rainbow trout and she was very happy little fisher person.

From Germany we returned to Alabama. We went back to the pond Kim caught bluegills before and we caught more bluegills. I bought a boat. It wasn't much of a boat, just a fourteen-foot jon boat with a seven and a half horse power outboard. I took the Kim, her sister Lisa and now brother Todd fishing for crappies. We found crappies in flooded timber and everyone caught fish. We took a break for lunch, roasting hot dogs over a wood fire on a rocky shore.

We moved to North Carolina after that, living in the Appalachian Mountains while I taught ROTC. The first spring we were there I took Kim, Lisa and Todd trout fishing on a small pond not far from the Blue Ridge Parkway. The kids fished with jigs below a bobber and they flipped their baits out, bringing them back with a slow retrieve. Suddenly a trout hit the jig and their rod was bent in half, fish swirling on the surface and then dragging the fish up on the bank. Kim, her sister, brother and I all ended the morning with our limits of brook trout.

Kim and I were much alike. We both had red hair and green eyes. Although we were born twenty-five years apart, our birthdays were separated by only two days on the calendar in mid December. She had lots of attitude and that was always one of her strong suits.

After a couple years I was alerted to another tour to Germany as I was finishing my third year in North Carolina. The kids needed to have Social Security Numbers to get passports so we applied for them. When we got the Social Security Cards it turned out Kim and I had the same last four numbers. What are the chances of a father and daughter having the same last four numbers from two different states, applied twenty years apart?

Kim was entering her teen years, starting high school when we arrived in Germany. Perhaps because we were so much alike, we seemed to delight in irritating each other. Of course, as a teen she barely tolerated the fact she and I breathed the same air. When we tangled, which seemed fairly often in those years, I told her we were much alike. She vehemently disputed that so I pointed out we both had red hair, green eyes, our birthdays were two days apart and we had the same last four numbers on our Social Security Card. With that she would just stomp off.

Those last years in Germany and the ones after we left were busy ones for her. Fishing fell by the wayside for her. In high school she played basketball and in her senior year she was co-captain of her girl's high school basketball team. When she graduated from high school, she was the class valedictorian. We moved to Minneapolis/Saint Paul for the last two years before I retired from the Army.

She and I survived her teen years. She grew up to be a beautiful, kind, smart, creative and strong women. She still had the attitude. She graduated from the University of Minnesota, eventually meeting and falling in love with a young man named Damien Aguilar. They married, had two children, a boy named Elijah and daughter Sophia and bought a large home in Minnetonka, a suburb on the western edge of the Twin Cities.

Kim and I hadn't fished together for a number of years when Damien mentioned to me, while we were ice fishing at Lake of the Woods, "I think Kim would like to go fly fishing with you." A few years before she and her sister had taken a woman in the outdoors workshop, signing up for fly fishing. I went into the basement, found a couple fly rods and gave one to each of them. We went to a little pond and practiced casting. She told me later she fly fished for bluegills a little bit off the dock at one of her friend's cabin but found it difficult while watching a couple young children.

It was an early summer day and I telephoned Kim "Are you busy Friday?" I asked.

"Not really," she told me.

"Can you put the kids in day care for the day?" I responded.

"Ya," she said. "Why?"

"Want to go fly fishing?"

She didn't hesitate. "Sure," she said as she laughed.

It was a blue skies, warm summer day when we arrived at a small lake in eastern side of Saint Croix County. As I pushed the boat off the trailer, I noticed little wind. A perfect day for fly fishing. At the landing I rigged two fly rods. We were fishing for panfish. We didn't need long, fancy leaders, using just a short five-foot section of four-pound monofilament. I attached a black foam bug pattern to both lines. I sat in front of the boat operating the trolling motor as we flipped our flies towards the brush in the water or trees overhanging from the bank.

When fly fishing for panfish you don't have to be too careful. They are not finicky and the objective is to just get the fly out in front, on the water close to any cover. It didn't take long before we heard a slight pop as a bluegill sucked in the fly. Kim pulled back on her fly rod, rod tip plunging as a bluegill fought against the rod as it made a short run. It came splashing to the surface as Kim brought the fish next to the boat. Kim had come a long way from the cane pole with kernels of corn.

The weather was pleasantly mild for an early summer day. The fish were hitting and in the next couple hours we caught a couple dozen orange bellied, brightly colored bluegills. We talked and laughed as we reminisced about things that happened as she grew up, the many places we lived and the people we met along the way. We remembered many of the early fishing trips we made when she was a child.

There was a swirl and a splash much larger than a bluegill could make and Kim's light fly rod bent double as a fish surged off. She stopped the fish, got it coming back toward the boat but the fish made a couple short runs. The fish strayed deep but eventually it was splashing next the boat when I leaned over the side and pulled in a foot long bass. She caught the only bass of the day and the biggest fish of the trip. It had been a wonderful day.

The next summer we both were busy. With young kids in sports and other activities, plus trying to squeeze family camping trips and travel, the summers seem to melt away. I realized we hadn't fished together. It was only a few days before school started and time was quickly disappearing. We found a day, with all the last-minute school preparations filling up the last few days, for her to bring her kids out to go fishing.

It was a windy day with bright skies and puffy white clouds being pushed around overhead. We were fishing a lake in Polk County, an hour drive north of my home in Hudson, Wisconsin. We went first to a small bay where I have seen people getting lots of bluegills. I dropped the anchor and we were now fishing spincasting outfits with balsam floats a couple feet up from ice jigs, baited with wax worms. Elijah was the oldest and had fished before so he knew how to cast. Sophia didn't have it down yet so Kim assisted in casting for her.

After fifteen minutes without a strike, we moved. One thing about fishing for panfish is if they don't hit within a few minutes, they obviously aren't there and you need to move. I motored the boat across the lake into a flat where I have seen schools of panfish but the wind made it difficult to keep the boat in place even with an anchor. We moved back to the other side of the lake where we had been and where the wind was skipping over the trees, leaving a thirty-to-forty-foot band of water free from the wind.

We anchored about twenty feet off the bank where a number of trees spread out over the water and in front of the trees there seemed to be a little deeper trench of water. Elijah casted his rod and Kim casted for Sophia and then handed her the rod. Immediately floats began to bounce and dip below the surface. Kim was coaching Sophia, telling her when she had a strike and giving her the finer points on setting the hook.

Both kids started catching fish. Sophia caught a couple large yellow perch as well as bluegills. I kept taking fish off hooks and Kim kept baiting Sophie's hooks while Eli baited his own hooks. Eli caught a foot long largemouth bass which was our trophy for the day. Fishing action was continuous until we ran out of bait. There was lots of laughter, whopping and hollering that afternoon. It was the perfect end to summer.

The kids went to school, there was the family

Thanksgiving hosted by Kim and Damien and then all the kids with their kids coming to our house for Christmas. Winter was full of more activities. Damien and I and a couple friends made our annual ice fishing trip to lake of the Woods. About six and a half months after Kim and I took her kids fishing before school started, Kim called my wife Becky and me. "I have bad news," she said. "I have been diagnosed with breast cancer."

I was shocked but had to get over it quickly. I needed to be positive for both of us. "Breast cancer is beatable," I told her.

"I know," she said.

"We will do whatever we need to do," I said.

There were more tests and visits to the doctor. I remember one afternoon when she curled up next to me on the sofa as I held her. It had been years since I last held her like that. Her doctors recommended chemo. Becky and I took her to weekly chemo treatments. The first couple treatments made her nauseous but her doctors and nurses made adjustments to her medications and after that she was able to go out for lunch after we finished chemo. It broke my heart a bit to see her lose that long, lovely red hair. But it will grow back. Becky and I sat with her while she was getting chemo and talked and laughed as we remembered various adventures or misadventures of her childhood, the dog we had, her friends who hung around our house and travels and moves we made.

The summer went by fast. On August 6 she had her last chemo. The doctors told her they couldn't find any tumors. She had beaten breast cancer. We were overjoyed. Kim hadn't much family time during the summer so she quickly booked a Disney Cruise for her, her husband and kids with a couple other friends. It was time to make up for time lost during the summer and to celebrate. Her hair was beginning to grow back. There were still some things to do when she got back. She still needed a double mastectomy since she carried the gene for breast cancer and then radiation but it would be done by Christmas with only reconstructive surgery early the following year. There was much to celebrate.

It was almost the end of August. The day was warm but not hot, sunny with bright blue skies and light winds. We had no concerns, no worries and a perfect day for fishing. Becky and I hooked up the boat, stopping at a small bar and grill for breakfast. When we got out to the car, heading north to the lake we wanted to fish, Becky looked at her cell phone. "I got a call from Kim," she said. Becky dialed back as I was driving. Kim answered the phone. "Things have changed drastically," she said. "The cancer has metastasized to my brain. We are abandoning all breast cancer treatments. I will start full brain radiation tomorrow." We were in shock. The cancer was supposed to be gone. How could this be possible?

A couple days earlier Kim was having headaches, double vision and felt unsteady on her feet. She went to the doctor. They did some testes and that morning she got the results.

I turned the car around as Becky continued to talk to Kim and we started back for home. There was no more interest in fishing. As I drove by the bar and grill where we had breakfast and didn't have a care in the world just a few minutes earlier I had tears in my eyes.

Becky and I took her every day for her treatments and now a grim reality set in. This was a fight for her life. She began wearing an eye patch to reduce the double vision.

Within a couple of weeks Kim lost her mobility. She needed help for personal care, she couldn't walk so we got a wheel chair, she got a ramp placed on the stairs to the house so we could get her in and out of the house. She needed help getting in and out of the wheel chair where ever she had to go. She needed care on a day-to-day basis. Becky and I became her care providers Monday through Friday until her husband came home from work.

Becky, Damien and I took her to the Mayo Clinic in Rochester, Minnesota. Her sister Lisa came up from her home in La Crosse. She had another battery of tests and scans to undergo before we could talk to the doctor. The doctor told us two things. First of all, the Mayo Clinic found the brain cancer in her initial PET scan earlier in the year. Then he told us he had a patient like Kim and they were able to put her cancer in remission for two years now. We had hope.

The Mayo doctors were working with Kim's doctors in Minneapolis. Physical and occupational therapy came to Kim's house. They gave her exercises to strengthen her legs and arms so she could walk again. Becky and I cleaned her house, did the laundry and shopping and helped her with her personal care and her exercises. We took her for chemo treatments once the radiation was completed.

Once a week we took her to lunch. After one lunch we went across the street to a couple of antique stores. I wheeled Kim through the tight aisles and as we went past one of the displays I saw a metal fly box. I opened it up and it had about a dozen flies in it. I showed it to Kim and told her I was going to buy it so next summer when all this was over and she was back to normal she and I would go fly fishing again for bluegills. She smiled and said "oh yes."

A month later we went back to the May Clinic and were told the tumors were shrinking? We were overjoyed. But, and there always seemed to be a but. They found cancer tumors in her lower spine. There was more radiation and then more chemo.

Kim fought back hard. She wasn't going to give in. She faced everyday with courage and a determined attitude. I remember holding her once as she cried, telling me she wanted to live long enough to see her kids grow up. She started to win. She finally was able to get out of bed and a chair by herself. She could use the bathroom by herself. By Thanksgiving she was able to walk with a walker and sometimes with a cane. She was getting stronger. Everything was looking up. She could now stay by herself during the day.

A week after Thanksgiving, my wife and I were leaving for our annual two-week trip to Key West. We talked about canceling the trip but Kim was doing so well and she said go. "I will be fine." She had friends and her husband's family nearby to help if she needed it. She had only a couple chemo treatments to do anyway while we were gone. Two days before we left, Becky and I took her to next chemo treatment. The nurses drew blood and then came out to tell us her blood numbers weren't right so they couldn't administer her chemo treatment. It will be fine, they assured us. There was nothing that could be done about the blood. They said her blood should be back to normal next week when she came back for her next chemo treatment.

We left for Key West but Kim was never far from our thoughts. We called her at least once a day. Everything was fine, she told us. She went for her next chemo and her numbers weren't right yet so they had to postpone her chemo for another week. Then she fell. She downplayed the fall, telling us she was alright.

Then in the last week we were in Key West she went into the hospital. Becky and I were checking to see if we could change our flights to earlier flights and come back early. Kim told us not to worry. There was nothing we could do any anyway. She was in the hospital and would be out in a couple days. We would be home shortly after that.

Two days after we got back to Wisconsin, Kim went back into the hospital again. Becky and I stayed the night with her. She was released from the hospital on Christmas Eve. She would have Christmas with Damien's family that evening, with her kids and husband the following day and a couple days later with the collected Yurk family. She was in a lot of pain but disregarded it the best she could so she could see the joy on her nephew and nieces faces. The next morning, she was having more difficulties so an ambulance was called. When we were in the emergency room, before the hospital could move her to an open room, the hospital doctor asked us if we had looked into hospice. Reality was catching up to us. There were tears in our eyes as we pondered that development. But one of her other doctors told us of a new treatment where they inserted chemo directly into Kim's spine.

That night I stayed with her and sometime in the early morning she woke. She looked at me and asked "why was everyone crying when I opened my eyes in the emergency room?" I couldn't lie to her. "They asked us about hospice," I said.

"Does this mean it is the end, Daddy?" She asked. Luckily, we had one more regimen of chemo treatments. "No, honey," I told her. "There is another series of chemo treatments yet." She closed her eyes and I kissed the top of her head. I didn't tell her if these next treatments didn't work there was nothing more her doctors could do.

She got the first treatment with another one scheduled in a few days. Becky and I didn't want her to be alone or afraid anytime she woke. She slept a lot but we didn't want her to be there by herself. Becky stayed with her during the days and I stayed with her at nights. There was a recliner type chair in her room and I pulled it next to her bed, stretched it out, sleeping fitfully next her, holding her hand at night. This cancer was aggressive and unrelenting. She would not get the next chemo treatment. It would not have helped the doctors said.

The next day she was moved to hospice. I spent the night sleeping in a chair next to her bed, holding her hand. She was unconscious. Twenty-eight hours after she first arrived at hospice she lost the battle. She was a month over forty-five years old, leaving behind a husband and two children ages eleven and eight as well as countless other family members and friends who loved her.

She was cremated. Her funeral was a week later on a cold, clear, windy January afternoon. The funeral home had to bring extra chairs into the hallway to accommodate all the people who were there. I was one of the people who gave eulogies. There was some laughter, Kim would have appreciated that, along with the tears. Winter came and went. Spring arrived and then the early summer. Becky and I were never far from our memories of Kim. She was in our hearts every day. We have a small black and gold ceramic heart with some of her ashes sitting on a table with a photo taken of her with a mischievous smile and her long, red hair.

It was early summer and a fishing buddy joined me for a day of fly fishing for panfish. I went into the basement, got out a fly rod and was putting a box of sponge bugs in a small case when I saw the fly box I bought that day with Kim at the antique shop. I threw it in the bag too.

I planned on fishing one of those flies, catch just a fish or two and then retire it but once on the lake I decided I was going to fish those flies all day. I started with a Royal Coachman pattern. It has always been one of my favorite flies. I watched as a bluegill came up, sucked in the fly and headed away. I pulled back on my fly rod and it sprung alive as the fish splashed on the surface while running off. I caught half a dozen fish with it, changed to an ant pattern, caught a few more fish and finally put on a bee pattern. They all caught fish and by the end of the day we caught and released over several dozen bluegills.

Throughout the day I felt connected to Kim. I used the flies she and I planned to use when we were going fly fishing that summer. Perhaps in some small way we were fishing together again. She has her long, beautiful red hair back, and no longer in pain or fear and we are enjoying a bright, warm summer day.

Printed in the United States
by Baker & Taylor Publisher Services